The Field Guide to
KNOTS

THE EXPERIMENT

BECAUSE EVERY BOOK IS A TEST OF NEW IDEAS

THE FIELD GUIDE TO KNOTS: *How to Identify, Tie, and Untie Over 80 Essential Knots for Outdoor Pursuits*

Copyright © 2015 Quid Publishing

The Experiment, LLC, 220 East 23rd Street, Suite 301, New York, NY 10010-4674,
www.theexperimentpublishing.com

The Experiment's books are available at special discounts when purchased in bulk for premiums and sales promotions as well as for fund-raising or educational use. For details, contact us at info@theexperimentpublishing.com.

Library of Congress Cataloging-in-Publication Data

Holtzman, Bob.
  The field guide to knots : how to identify, tie, and untie over 80 essential knots for outdoor pursuits / Bob Holtzman.
      pages cm
  Includes index.
  ISBN 978-1-61519-276-2 (hardcover) -- ISBN 978-1-61519-277-9 (ebook)
  1. Knots and splices--Handbooks, manuals, etc. I. Title.
  VM533.H64 2015
  623.88'82--dc23
                          2015019181

ISBN 978-1-61519-276-2
Ebook ISBN 978-1-61519-277-9

Conceived, designed, and produced by, Quid Publishing, Part of the Quarto Group, Level 4 Sheridan House, 114 Western Road, Hove BN3 1DD - www.quidpublishing.com
Design by Rehab

Knots on front cover are, clockwise from left: Flemish Bend, Sheet Bend, Figure 8 Knot, Carrick Bend, and Bowline. Knots on back cover are, from top down: Cleat Hitch, Slipped Half Hitch, Alpine Coil, Mooring Hitch.

Main cover image © Bob Holtzman; icons © Shutterstock; back cover images © Feather Weight

Printed in China
Distributed by Workman Publishing Company, Inc.
Distributed simultaneously in Canada by Thomas Allen & Son Ltd.

First printing September 2015
10 9 8 7 6 5 4 3 2 1

This one's for the Maine Canoe Symposium, the Penobscot Paddle & Chowder Society,
and all my canoeing friends
B.H.

Acknowledgments

Thanks for the loans of various materials, and for suggestions of helpful knots, to: Sandie and Brendan Sabaka; Tim Barker and Ed Eaton of Maine Sport; and Shawn Burke. Rachel Styer of Feather Weight did a great job shooting the massive photography program and keeping it organized, and was a pleasure to work with. Plus scones. Can't forget the scones.

The Field Guide to
KNOTS

HOW TO IDENTIFY, TIE, AND UNTIE
OVER 80 ESSENTIAL KNOTS FOR OUTDOOR PURSUITS

Bob Holtzman
author of *Wilderness Survival Skills*

THE EXPERIMENT
New York

Contents

Introduction

Why *This* Knot Book?

Knot tying is an essential outdoor skill. Knots are indispensible to backpackers, climbers, boaters, and anglers. And anyone who spends time in the backcountry—including day hikers, birdwatchers, hunters, cross-country skiers, snowshoers, equestrians, and mountain bikers—should have basic knot-tying skills for everyday and emergency situations. And really, just about everyone has to tie stuff up on occasion, and doing it right makes the job quicker, easier, neater, and safer.

But there are already a lot of knot books out there, so what makes this one different? Three things:

1. It's designed to allow you to identify most functional knots you're likely to encounter in outdoor activities. That's what makes the book a "field guide."

2. The book explains how to *untie* each knot. That's more important than it may seem. Whether you need to change a sail, reposition a loop on a climbing rope, tighten a sagging dining fly, or splice a broken tent pole, untying knots is often the first step. Doing it correctly will make the job go faster and may reduce damage to the rope.

3. It provides an efficient way to select the right knot for any job. Rather than making you read lengthy descriptions of dozens of knots to find one that's appropriate, this book provides a quick overview of every knot at the beginning of each part, so you can quickly zero in on the one that best suits your needs.

Of course, the book explains how to tie the knots and includes alternate methods for a few of them. It also gives you the information you need to select the right kind of rope and it explains how to use it efficiently, and how to keep it in good condition. Good rope is expensive, and if you're using it in situations where personal safety is at stake, you want to know you can depend on it.

How to Use This Book

Just as a field guide to birds is organized by categories (wading birds, perching birds, hawks, etc.), the knots in this book are organized into categories. Whether you need to untie an existing knot or select a new knot for a job, the way to begin is to identify the knot or define your requirement by general type—binding knots, hitches, loop knots, etc.—and then narrow the search to the specific knot. On p.20 you will find information about the main categories of knots and what they're used for.

Once you know the category of knot you're looking at, or that you need to tie, turn to the part of the book that covers that category in detail. Each part begins with an identification key, consisting of photographs of every knot in the category, accompanied by a brief list of the knot's common uses. You will also find pro-and-con comments that compare a given knot to others in the category, in terms of security, ease of tying or untying, and other need-to-know information. Each photo is keyed to the page where tying and untying instructions are found, along with a more detailed description of the knot and its uses.

Like any other skill, knotting has special terminology, but the lexicon is pretty small and easily learned. It is much easier to read and follow instructions that use precise, concise terms rather than long descriptions. So be sure to read the first two sections of Part Two (beginning on p.46). As soon as you begin tying your first knots, these terms will all become familiar friends.

Knowing how to tie the right knot for every job is a useful—sometimes essential—outdoor skill. But it's also fun, gratifying, and very impressive when you can quickly rig a safety line for a climber, lash a canoe onto a car, or put up a tarp that stays up while others are struggling and flailing with tangled lines and knots that don't hold. Start by learning just a few knots in each category, and you may find yourself coming back for more.

Introduction

What Knots Are Included?

Of literally thousands of knots and similar ropework devices known for many purposes, there are 87 (including variations) in this book. How did we decide which to include? Well, this is a practical guide for outdoors enthusiasts, and the knots here are practical in the sense that each of them work well for a number of outdoor situations, and they're relatively easy to learn, tie, and remember.

Of course, this book includes knots in all the main categories, including stopper knots, binding knots, loop knots, bends, and hitches. Knots that are designed to make up bundles or packages (binding knots) are not appropriate for making connections between two objects with a section of rope (as when tying an anchor line, for which you'd want a hitch). And within categories, there are knots that are fine-tuned to more specific tasks—for example, loops that are adjustable versus loops with a fixed size, or knots that trade off ease of tying for greater security.

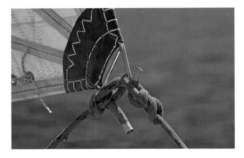

Other categories include lashings, whippings, seizings, and coils. Some of these are not knots per se, but they all involve knots and they are all essential ropework skills for the outdoors.

Just as backpackers select gear that serves more than one purpose in order to reduce weight in their packs, we prefer rope skills that can be used in many ways, to avoid filling our overburdened memory banks with a lot of single-purpose information. Most of the knots chosen are practical for a variety of outdoor activities, equally useful for camping, boating, climbing, fishing, wilderness living, and survival. For the same reason, there are no knots that are purely decorative. Decorative knotting is a fine hobby, but that simply isn't an objective of this book.

Most of the knots here are primarily for tying in twisted- or braided-fiber ropes. A few of them also work well in monofilament fishing line, webbing, leather straps, or bungee cord, but none of them are limited to these materials. None of them are appropriate to wire rope.

Finally, all the knots here can be tied without tools and without unlaying (i.e., untwisting) the strands or undoing the braids from which the rope is constructed. The only "special" material introduced is whipping thread, which is used to prevent the ends of rope from unraveling, and the whipping and seizing techniques shown do not require the use of a needle or sailmaker's palm.

Why So Many Knots?

It's one thing to say that a binding knot is appropriate for tying up a package and a hitch is a way to tie two things together with a section of rope in between. It's another to understand why there are different knots for different tasks. Even the simplest knot has more than a dozen characteristics that determine how well it will work in a given application:

Complexity: How many steps are involved? How difficult is it to learn and remember?

Ease of tying: Quite separate from its complexity, how difficult or time-consuming is it to tie?

Ease of untying: After it's been tightened, can it be untied with ease?

Security: Will the knot stay tied if the rope is pulled even tighter? Will it stay tied if the knot isn't tied very tight? Even if the knot remains tied, will it slip? (If it's a loop knot, will the size of the loop change? If it's a hitch, will it shift relative to the object it's tied to?)

Security under shock load: Will it remain secure if the rope is subjected to a sharp jerk? How about if it's shaken repeatedly, like on a flag halyard?

Adjustability: After it's tied, can the knot be made tighter or looser? Larger or smaller?

Adaptability to various sizes and materials: Can it be tied effectively in both thin and thick rope? In flat materials? With ropes made from both natural and synthetic fibers? How will these differences affect its security, ease of untying, etc.?

Ability to bind tight: Can the knot be tied tightly to or around another object? (Think about needing another thumb in order to tie up a package tightly.)

Ability to bind loose: Can the knot be tied securely but loosely around another object? (Think about a loop in the end of a rope that you might drop over the top of a post, but that you do not want to tighten around the post when you pull the rope tight.)

Retention of rope strength: All knots weaken rope, but some not as much as others.

Amount of rope required: Some knots require a lot; others not so much.

Bulk: How big is the finished knot? Will it interfere with the movement of the rope or the object to which it's tied?

How many ends are required? Some knots can be tied only if both ends of the rope are free. Others require only one end, and some can be tied "on the bight," in the middle of the rope with neither end free.

With so many variables to consider, it's not surprising that practitioners of different trades and outdoor pursuits created knots that combined exactly those characteristics suitable to the task at hand.

Introduction

General Guidelines for Tying Knots

None of the knots here are particularly complicated, but even so, it's pretty easy to get them wrong if you make a simple mistake, like passing one part of the rope *over* another when you should be passing it *under*. Relying on both text and images, carefully follow instructions step by step, paying close attention to *over* versus *under*, *left* versus *right, working end* versus *standing part*, and the direction of loops (i.e., clockwise or counterclockwise, overhand or underhand). These terms are explained on pp.17–19.

If a knot doesn't come out right, untie it completely and start from the beginning, making sure each step is done exactly as shown.

Sometimes a correctly tied knot won't look like the photograph, in which case, it will simply need to be faired, i.e., worked into shape by some careful rearrangement. See p.23 for directions on finishing and fairing knots.

All knots can be tied upside down or as mirror images of the examples. When learning how to tie a knot upside down from the way it's pictured, you can simply turn the book upside down and follow the photos in the normal order. To tie a knot that's a mirror image of the photo (in which left and right are reversed), you can view the pictures in a mirror. Remember that when you do such a reversal, some *but not all* of the following directional pairs may need to be reversed as well: left/right, up/down, over/under, overhand/underhand, and clockwise/counterclockwise.

There's more than one way to tie most knots to produce identical results. The choice of an alternate method may be merely a matter of preference, or it may be dictated by the situation. This book provides alternate methods for a few knots, but different approaches may work just as well for almost any of them.

Rope comes in many varieties and sizes, and some knots don't work well with all kinds of rope. Twisted ("laid") rope kinks more readily than braided rope if looped in the wrong direction. Large-diameter rope may not take kindly to being bent into a small radius. Some synthetic ropes are too slippery to hold certain knots securely. And ropes of greatly different sizes or different materials may not knot together easily or effectively. See pp.25–32 to learn how to select rope that's appropriate to your needs.

It's one thing to tie a knot with the book in front of you on the kitchen table—it's another to tie it when you need it in a real-world situation. The key to truly learning a knot is memorization through repetition and practice. After you've tied a knot a few times using the book, try doing it from memory. Then try again in an hour, and again the following day. With the exception of the simplest knots, chances are that you may forget the procedure. But tie that knot from memory every day for a week, and you'll own it. Then, when you need a knot fast, you'll be able to do it confidently and correctly, regardless of conditions.

Safety

Personal safety in outdoor activities can depend upon good rope and well-tied knots. Climbers carefully inspect their ropes and habitually check each other's knots to guard against mistakes. If you don't have access to experienced backup, it's important to check your own knots scrupulously before relying on them. If you're unsure about a particular knot, it may be safer to substitute one in which you have total confidence, even if it might be less convenient.

Broken fibers indicate that this rope is well past its useful life for any purpose where safety is at stake

The safe working load of most rope is printed on the package. It's usually considerably lower than the breaking strength

The condition of the rope itself is also of key concern. Just sitting on a shelf, almost all ropes will deteriorate with age, and wear accelerates with use and exposure to the elements. Inspect any rope inch by inch before using it in a safety-related application. Signs of excessive wear or age include: fraying, permanent kinks, discoloration, broken or melted fibers, reduced diameter, the cover sliding over the core, and areas where the angle of the lay or braid changes.

"Breaking strength" is the load at which a rope breaks under laboratory conditions, when brand new and under steadily increasing load. This figure may not be readily available to the consumer, but working load—the maximum load to which the manufacturer recommends the rope be subjected—is usually printed on the packaging, or on the reel in stores where rope is sold by the foot or meter.

Introduction

The working load is usually in the range of 15–25 percent of the breaking strength. This may seem overly cautious, but in fact it's merely prudent. Most rope becomes weaker when wet, and many knots reduce the strength of rope by half, so as soon as you tie a knot, the rope's margin of safety (the difference between its actual breaking strength and the working load) could drop from 4:1 to about 2:1. The working load also allows a reasonable safety margin considering the age of the rope, its wear, and, to an extent, any shock loads (sharp jerks) it has absorbed. Any rope that has been subjected to a really heavy shock load should be retired from use where safety is an issue, and used henceforth only in non-critical applications.

Ropes in long-term outdoor static use (such as securing tarps over boats or stacked firewood) are exposed to sunshine and frequent cycles of wet/dry and freeze/thaw, and they pick up blown dust. All of these shorten a rope's lifespan. Cheap polypropylene rope is particularly subject to degradation from UV exposure, which can make the fibers brittle in a matter of weeks. These kinds of commonplace uses are a good way to re-use high-quality rope that has reached the end of its safe working life in more critical applications.

Climbing ropes have details permanently marked with end labels

Many ropes—including all modern climbing ropes—are constructed in two (occasionally three) layers, with a central strength member or core composed of (usually) twisted strands, covered by a braided mantle (also known as a sheath or cover) that protects the core from abrasion and provides a good gripping surface. The core of a climbing rope may be weakened or damaged due to arresting a fall, while the mantle remains intact.

Because this kind of damage can't be readily detected by visual inspection, it is essential to follow the manufacturer's guidelines on when to retire a climbing rope. To abide by these guidelines, it's important to record rope use in a logbook, noting the date of manufacture, the date first put into use, the type of use, the duration of each use, the cumulative amount of time used, the number of climbs, the height of any falls arrested, and any known damage.

Safety

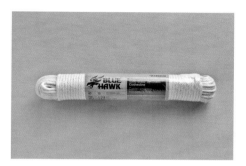

Clothesline is inexpensive but weak. Do not use it in any application where safety is at stake

If you've ever seen a boat airborne over a highway, chances are it was "secured" to the vehicle with either clothesline or bungee cords. Clothesline is cheap and ubiquitous, but it is not adequate for any application involving safety. Don't use it to tie up boats, protect against falls, lift heavy loads, or secure cargo to a motor vehicle or trailer. Bungee cords are useful to fasten tarps over stacked material, control slack, or form a temporary bundle, but they should never be used to secure large or heavy loads.

It bears repeating: **test every knot before relying on it for safety.** Improperly tied knots—and properly tied knots that aren't right for the job—can slip or untie themselves unexpectedly, with potentially life-threatening results. Use this book to learn basic knot-tying skills, but seek expert advice in situations where personal safety is at stake.

Never use bungee cords to secure loads to a car's roof rack

Part One
Rope and Knot Basics

Anatomy and Taxonomy

Everyone knows what "rope," "string," and "cord" mean, even if the exact definitions and distinctions between these types of cordage or "stuff" (the most general and inclusive terms) can be a little fuzzy. Even professional ropeworkers and riggers differ sometimes in their use of terminology. Nonetheless, the following definitions are generally accepted:

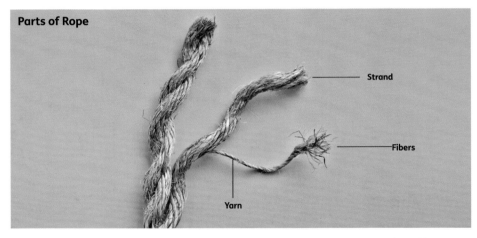

Parts of Rope

Strand

Fibers

Yarn

Fiber: the smallest component from which cordage is made. In a natural fiber rope, it would be the hair-thin stuff, more or less, as it comes from the plant, like a fiber from a cotton boll or coconut husk. In synthetic rope, it's a single filament of nylon, polypropylene, or similar material.

Yarn: made from twisted fibers; often about the diameter of sewing thread.

Strand: made from twisted yarns. Most laid ropes consist of three strands twisted together. This book also uses strand in a non-technical

sense in the knot-tying instructions, to distinguish one section of a rope or knot from another, as in "take the left strand of the crossing turn and cross it over the right strand."

Rope: the most common weight of cordage used for knots in outdoor use, typically ⅜ in. (9 mm) or greater in diameter.

Line: a non-specific term for a rope when it's in use, especially on boats. Take a piece of rope and use it to raise a sail, and it's suddenly a line. This book will use the terms "rope"

and "line" interchangeably.

Hawser: the same as a rope, but the term is generally used only for ropes that are twisted into cables (see below). Somewhat confusingly, it can also mean a very heavy line used for towing, mooring, anchoring, or tying up large ships, in which case, the line probably *is* a length of cable.

Cable: very heavy stuff made up of three twisted hawsers. Not typically used outside of industrial applications and ships.

Working Terms and Basic Shapes

Without some basic knot-tying jargon, instructions would be impossibly long and convoluted. We will use most of these terms repeatedly throughout the book.

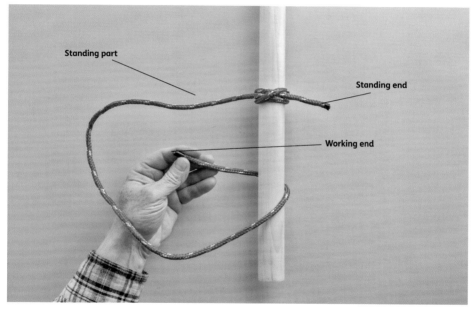

Working end, working part, or running end: the free end of a rope manipulated in tying a knot.

Standing end, standing part: the end of the rope that is not fully subject to manipulation in knot tying. Often, it is already fastened to something else. The standing part is the length of rope facing the standing end and not subject to manipulation.

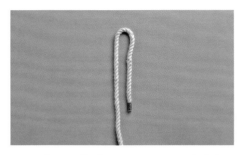

Bight: a sharp small-radius curve in a rope in which the working and standing parts are brought near to or in contact with one another. It can also mean any part of the rope other than the ends. A knot that is tied "on the bight" is tied somewhere in the middle, without manipulation of either end.

Bitter end: the last inch or two of a rope—too short a section to really work with.

Loop: somewhat like a bight, but the curve is of a larger radius and it encloses more area. The term also describes the part of a loop knot or other rope structure that completely encircles an object.

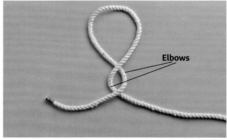

Crossing turn: a curve in which the rope crosses over itself once. If you twist a bight 180 degrees, a crossing turn is the result.

Elbow: Take a bight and twist it 360 degrees: the elbows are the two sections of rope between the crossing turn at the top, and the working end and standing part at the bottom.

Working Terms and Basic Shapes

Overhand and underhand: a crossing turn in which the working end is over the standing part is known as "overhand," as in the photo below. An "underhand" crossing turn is the opposite, where the working end is under the standing part, as in the photo above. The crossing turn may be above or below the run of the rope. If you turn an overhand crossing turn over, it becomes underhand.

Loopy Confusion

The meaning of "loop" is subject to disagreement among ropeworkers. Some consider a loop to be the same as our definition of a crossing turn. Others say the rope must cross over itself twice to be considered a loop (as shown in the photograph of an elbow on the page opposite). In the step-by-step instructions in this book, a loop is an arrangement in which the rope encloses more area than a bight, and does not cross itself. We also occasionally use "loop" in a more common sense to mean any rope formation that can enclose an object and that's more permanent than a crossing turn, like the loop in a loop knot.

Clockwise and counterclockwise: another aspect of the direction of a crossing turn. Follow the rope around the turn from the standing part toward the working end. The direction of the curve will be either clockwise or counterclockwise (in the case of the photo above, it's counterclockwise). If you turn a clockwise crossing turn over, it becomes counterclockwise.

Turn: a half-revolution of rope around a post or other fixed object, so that both ends face the same direction and the object is not completely encircled (see 1. above).

Round turn: a full revolution of rope around an object. The rope may wind 360 degrees around the object, so ends face in opposite directions (2.), or it may wind 540 degrees around, so that ends face the same direction (3.). If the object is to be encircled by several adjacent round turns (4.), each revolution is referred to as a "wrap."

Types of Knots

Almost any rope formation that is used to fasten, tighten, attach, or constrain the rope itself or other objects can be called a knot. Stopper knots, loop knots, bends, and hitches are all knots in this general sense. (Whippings and seizings are not considered knots even in this general sense of the word, and the status of lashings and coils is somewhat ambiguous.) But *knot* also has a more specific technical meaning, being a formation in which a rope is tied *to itself* rather than to another object.

Knots in the general sense are divided into categories based upon how they are used. The following definitions not only describe the subsequent organization of the book, they also serve as guidance to identifying an existing knot or selecting the right category of knot for your needs.

Foundation knots: this is an ad hoc category that introduces some of the most basic knots and concepts, all of which are used repeatedly throughout the book. See Part Two (p.46).

Stopper knots: "true" knots, in which the rope is tied to itself to create a structure—usually at an end—that prevents it from escaping through a narrow opening, adds weight that allows it to be thrown, or serves as a handhold. See Part Three (p.58).

Binding knots: true knots in which the rope is tied to itself to tightly enclose or bind together another object or objects. See Part Four (p.74).

Types of Knots

Loop knots: true knots in which the rope is tied to itself to form a closed loop that can be placed around an object (like a post), or to which an object can be connected (like a carabiner). Loop knots may fit loosely or tightly around the object and the size of the loop may be adjustable (known as sliding loops or nooses) or fixed. See Part Five (p.86).

Bends: rope structures that tie the ends of two ropes together. Not true knots. See Part Six (p.116).

Hitches: rope structures that tie a rope to an object such as a ring or a post, usually at one end. (The other end is generally tied to something else, like a boat or a tarp.) Hitches are not true knots, as they are tied *to* the object and depend upon it for part of their structure, whereas a loop knot is freestanding and independent of the object it surrounds. See Part Seven (p.138).

Lashings: considered by some ropeworkers to be in a special class of *binding knots*, these rope structures generally incorporate numerous round turns or wraps, to tie two or more poles tightly together when building a structure. See Part Eight (p.160).

Part One: Rope and Knot Basics

Whipping: a tight wrapping of heavy thread or small cord around the end of a rope, to prevent it from unraveling. A whipping is not a knot, even in the general sense. See Part Nine (p.179).

Seizing: a tight wrapping of heavy thread or small cord around two sections of rope, used to join two ropes end-to-end, or to form an eye (a permanent loop) in the end or in a bight of a single rope. Like whippings, seizings are not knots. See Part Nine (p.179).

Coil: an arrangement of rope that keeps it orderly and prevents it from tangling during storage or transportation (see photo on right). As a measure of basic rope care, coils are covered in this part of the book, beginning on p.37.

Splice: a structure in which the strands of a rope are separated and then woven together in order to: terminate the end of a rope to keep it from unraveling; form an eye in the end of a rope; or join two ropes end-to-end. A splice is not a knot: it is not tied, and it is considered permanent and never to be undone. Splices are not covered in this book.

When a Knot's Not a Knot

Because ropework developed as folk craft within different trades in different places, and at different times, there's much inconsistency in terminology, extending to the very names of knots themselves. (We couldn't really expect a Scottish shepherd, a Massachusetts whaler, and an Oklahoma wheat farmer to agree on terms, could we?) And some knots can be used in more than one way. Hence, a Blood Knot is really a bend, the Fisherman's Bend is actually a hitch, and a Square Knot is tied as a bend as often as it's used as a binding knot. So don't be surprised to find a knot name in what appears to be the wrong part of the book.

Finishing Knots

If a knot is tied correctly but lacks the expected form or symmetry, it can often be "faired"—worked into shape or rearranged without untying. If the knot you've tied looks out of shape, examine the photo of the finished knot and see if you can replicate it simply by pushing or pulling various parts of the knot relative to others. Fairing a knot is not only a matter of aesthetics: an improperly formed knot may also be insecure.

1.

2.

3.

4.

5.

If the knot has too much slack, it can generally be worked back through the knot in either direction—toward the standing part or toward the working end. This may or may not be easier than untying the knot and starting again. If you've already pulled the knot tight, you will probably have to loosen it first. If a knot simply won't tighten, you may be pulling the wrong part. This is especially common with loop knots and bends, where there are usually three or four parts to choose from. The sequence on this page shows an untidy knot (1.) being faired by first loosening it (2., 3.), then rearranging and retightening its parts (4., 5.) without actually untying it.

Untying Knots

The process of untying most knots is simple in theory: you identify the working end, loosen whatever is holding it in place, and then thread the working end through whatever else is holding it in place until it's completely free.

In practice, though, many knots are difficult to untie after they've been put to use. Once tightened, they become like Chinese puzzles in which you can't loosen Part A until Part B is loose, but Part B is held tight by Part C, which is held down by Part A. This isn't accidental: it's key to the tremendous security of many knots.

There's usually a solution, though, and each knot in this book has instructions for untying it. There are a few knots, however, that just can't be untied readily (especially if tied in really small stuff like monofilament fishing line) and have to be cut. This is something to consider before you tie a knot.

The Square Knot is easy to untie. Grab one bight in each hand and pull in opposite directions.

The Angler's Loop is very difficult to untie, and often must be cut.

Buying Rope

There are dozens of factors to consider when buying rope for a specific purpose. One has to consider how it's going to be used—the environment it will be used in and the stresses it will incur—and weigh that against the performance characteristics of different kinds of rope. These factors are summarized in the table below.

Usage Considerations	
Static versus dynamic uses	Will the rope pretty much stay put when it's in use (as when securing a bundle) or will it be in motion (controlling a sail, for example)? Will it rub against rough surfaces, making abrasion resistance important? Is stretch desirable (for example, to absorb shock loads) or undesirable?
Strength and safety margin	What continuous and shock loads will it be subject to? How large a margin of safety is required?
Knotting requirements	What kind of knots are required? Will the rope be tied tightly or loosely, and will it be tied to itself, to other ropes, or to other objects? Will the required knots force the rope into small-radius curves, and will they diminish the strength of the rope significantly?
Friction	Is it desirable or undesirable that the rope slides easily against itself or against other objects? Will it be handled frequently? If so, will it offer sufficient grip without excessive roughness?
Environmental exposure	Will the rope be exposed to sunlight for a long time? Will it be wet when it's in use? Will it remain wet for long periods? Will it be exposed to high heat, oil, or other chemicals?
Weight and size	Is a large diameter desirable for easy gripping, or a small diameter for easier knotting? What length of rope is needed? How much space and weight-carrying capacity is available for storage and transportation?
Buoyancy	Some ropes float and others sink in water. Is either characteristic relevant to your application?
Appearance	Are bright, easily recognized colors desirable, or is it preferable that the rope blends in with its surroundings?

Rope Variables	
Type of fiber	Numerous choices of natural and synthetic fibers
Construction	Laid, braided, and combination designs
Diameter	Directly affects strength; also influences knotting
Resistance to UV, heat, rot, chemicals	A factor of fiber type and chemical coatings or treatments
Breaking strength and working load	A factor of construction, fiber type, and diameter
Stretch	A factor of construction and fiber type
Durability	A factor of construction and fiber type
Price	(Of course)

Part One: Rope and Knot Basics

There's also a subjective factor in rope selection. You may simply prefer how a certain type of rope feels and how it knots. For knot-tying practice, buy a variety of rope types in short lengths: 10–12 ft. (3–3.75 m) of each should do it. Get a feel for them and form your own opinions.

Estimating Length

How much cordage to buy, how much to bring into the outdoors, and how much you'll need for a particular job all involve different calculations. In the long run, cordage tends to get used, so when you're purchasing rope by the foot or meter, it's often a good idea to buy more than your immediate needs. You might not know right now how you'll use the rest, but you can be pretty confident that you will use it.

How much to bring with you, though, isn't so easy. Backpacks, bikes, horses, boats, and recreational vehicles have limited carrying capacity, so you'll have to estimate how much rope you might need between resupply opportunities, and balance that against how much you can comfortably carry. Plan on having enough to cover only likely emergencies and rope failures, not every conceivable emergency under the sun. Sailing imposes heavy demands on rope, and it is neither practical nor safe to use undersized, understrength cordage, but no sailor has ever had to replace all his stays, shrouds, halyards, sheets, and anchor rodes on a single passage. One hundred feet (30 m) of good-quality parachute cord is small and light and will suffice for most situations that a backpacker is likely to encounter (excluding rescues). Bottom line: be prepared, not paranoid.

On the other hand, almost any given job requires more rope than you think. Knots use up a lot of inches, and the thicker the rope, the more a knot requires. Every time you pass a rope around an object, you have to account for still more length. And you need enough extra rope at the end of a knot to have something to grab onto to pull it tight. As a rule of thumb, make an initial estimate, then add a fudge factor of 25 percent.

On the other hand, having too much rope for a particular job has drawbacks too. Longer rope is more likely to become tangled, and most knots will take longer to tie if you have to pull an excessive amount of rope through every manipulation. When you've finished the knot, you may be left with a lot of extra rope. If you leave it there, it might be in the way. If you choose to cut extra rope off, then you have at least one more rope end to whip and possibly a length of rope remaining that's too short to be of any practical use—in other words, a waste.

Uncoiling New Rope

Cordage must be removed from packaging correctly to avoid creating kinks. Rope that is sold on reels must be unrolled, never lifted off the end of the reel as needed. Pass a rod or dowel through the middle of the reel and support it horizontally, so that the reel rotates freely as you pull the rope off from the top. Cordage that is sold in hollow coils or balls (usually contained within a box, for rope, or plastic wrap, for twine) must be lifted out from the center of the coil, with the cordage being taken from the bottom of the coil. Packaged hanks of rope, in which coils are compressed by multiple round turns, should be treated like a reel: the hank should be rotated on its long axis to unwind the round turns until the coils are exposed.

Rope Construction and Materials

Cordage derives its performance characteristics from the type of fiber used and the design or method of construction. The fibers from which a rope is made may be natural (e.g., cotton) or synthetic (e.g., nylon). Virtually all natural fiber and most synthetic fiber ropes consist of a single type of fiber, but some synthetic ropes combine more than one type of fiber.

Fibers, yarns, and strands may be either twisted or braided together to make rope. The vast majority of natural fiber ropes are twisted, while synthetic fiber ropes are about equally divided between the two types of construction.

Many synthetic ropes are built in two layers, with an inner core and outer cover, jacket, sheath, or mantle (see right). This kind of construction, common in climbing ropes, is known as kernmantle, from the German for "core" and "jacket." In these ropes, the core is the main strength member, while the cover protects the core from abrasion and environmental wear and provides a comfortable gripping surface. The two need not be of the same construction. Ropes with braided covers may have braided cores, twisted cores, or even cores of straight, untwisted yarns; different materials may be selected for their different performance characteristics.

Inner core (white) and outer cover (blue)

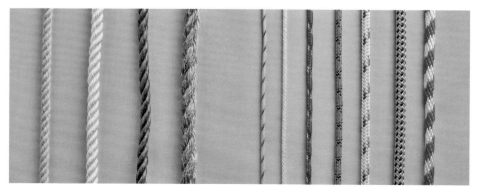

A selection of twisted (left) and braided (right) ropes

Natural Versus Synthetic Fibers

Until the invention of plastics, all ropes (other than wire ropes) were made of natural fibers. In different times and places, these have included both animal and vegetable fibers. Animal fibers used in ropework have included rawhide, leather, wool, and many types of animal and human hair, but none of these is in common use anymore. The exceptions are "catgut" (or simply "gut") and silk. Catgut is actually derived from the intestines of barnyard animals such as sheep, goats, and cattle, and its use in cordage is almost entirely limited to medical sutures, racket strings, and strings for musical instruments. Silk is also used for sutures and for thread that goes into fine fabrics and rugs. Although silk is extremely strong, it is never used for any but decorative ropes, because of its high cost. With plant fibers being so much cheaper and more abundant, it is no surprise that they became the norm for industrial-scale ropemaking, and when speaking of natural fiber ropes, vegetable fiber is a given.

Plastics first came into practical use in the 20th century, and the ability to extrude or draw molten plastic into fibers presented a new raw material for ropemaking that was not only cheaper than natural fibers, but had several performance advantages as well. As economies of scale took hold and new plastics were developed, synthetic ropes quickly gained market share and came to dominate most uses. Natural fiber ropes accordingly declined in popularity, and some have fallen out of use altogether except for very limited niche or artisanal applications.

Natural Versus Synthetic Fiber Ropes

Characteristic	Natural fiber rope	Synthetic fiber rope
Construction	Mostly twisted	Twisted or braided
Strength	Low to medium	Medium to very high
Stretch	Low to high	Low to high
Knot-holding ability	Medium to high	Low to high
Durability	Low to medium	Medium to very high
Appearance	Traditional	Traditional or modern
Color	White, tan or brown	Any
Surface, texture	Hairy (may be soft or bristly)	Not hairy (may be soft or hard)
Buoyancy	Sinks (except coir)	Sinks or floats
Chemical resistance	Low to medium	Low to very high
Rot resistance	Low to medium	Very high
Sun/heat/UV resistance	Low to high	Very low to very high
Price	Low to medium	Low to very high

Natural Versus Synthetic Fibers

Natural fiber Rope

With few exceptions (cotton clothesline being one of them), natural fiber ropes are of twisted construction. In some diameters they are the least expensive option, but for a given size, even the best natural fiber ropes tend to be weaker than the cheapest synthetic ones. Compared to synthetics, natural fibers are less durable and they degrade more quickly from most types of environmental exposure. On the other hand, all natural fiber ropes hold knots well, while many synthetic ropes are slippery and difficult to keep tied.

Although some natural fiber ropes will float in water briefly, all of them except coir will sink once they become saturated. Water absorption makes natural fiber ropes heavy, causes them to swell, and makes knots difficult to untie. Even while they swell, many natural fiber ropes will also shrink lengthwise when wet. Unlike synthetics, natural fibers are subject to rot. While this is usually a drawback, biodegradability can be an advantage in some situations.

Aside from their superior knot-holding qualities, the main advantages of natural fibers tend to be in the areas of look and feel. They can be used to present a rustic, natural appearance on traditional boats and as safety barriers and handholds on trails and in camps and cabins. While some synthetic ropes mimic this traditional look convincingly, it often comes at a higher price. Some find the feel of natural rope more pleasing too, although some natural fibers are softer than others, and some are quite coarse.

Manila

Manila comes from the abacá plant *(Musa textillis)*, a species of banana. Along with hemp, it is the strongest of the natural fiber ropes, but manila's resistance to rot and saltwater damage is superior. It was once commonly used for ships' hawsers (anchor lines) and fishing nets. Manila holds knots well and shrinks when wet, causing knots to tighten further: this can be advantageous in some applications and undesirable in others.

Hemp

With a smooth texture much like linen, hemp is the equal to manila as the strongest of the natural fibers used in ropemaking. Prior to the introduction of synthetics, it was the most popular rope for heavy-duty applications. (Ships were rigged largely with hemp rope, which was tarred to prevent rot.) It holds knots well but is subject to fairly high stretch. It comes from *Cannabis sativa*, the same plant that is the source of marijuana. But smoking a piece of hemp rope won't get you high; industrial farmers have bred the ropemaking variety for strength, not psychoactive properties.

Sisal

The fiber of the sisal plant *(Agave sisalana)* is among the stronger of the natural fibers, with good durability and medium to high stretch. Sisal twine is inexpensive and is still in common use for baling hay and general package tying. Heavier stuff exhibits the same good properties but is hard to find. The fiber henequen, which comes from another species of the same plant genus *(Agave fourcroydes)*, was once a common cordage fiber. It is not as strong as sisal and is almost never used in modern ropemaking. (A third member of the genus, *Agave tequilana* or blue agave, is used to make tequila which, although it is not cordage, can still be used to "tie one on.")

Cotton

The world's most popular fiber, cotton is smooth and soft. Cotton rope holds knots well and is easy to work with, but it is rather lacking for serious outdoor use (with the exception of clothesline, for which it is common). Strength and durability are very poor, stretch is very high, and it rots quickly.

Part One: Rope and Knot Basics

Natural Fiber Ropes Compared

Characteristic	Manila	Hemp	Sisal	Cotton	Jute	Coir
Strength	Very high	Very high	High	Very low	Low	Very low
Stretch	Medium to high	Medium to high	Medium to high	Very high	High	Very high
Texture/feel	Smooth	Smooth, hard	Soft, hairy	Very soft	Brittle	Coarse
Floats?	No	No	No	No	No	Yes
Durability and environmental resistance	Low	Low	Very low	Low	Low	Low
Price	Medium to high	High, not readily available	Low	Low	Low	Low, not readily available

Jute

Derived from plants of the genus *Corchorus*, jute is the world's second-largest fiber crop (after cotton). It is very inexpensive and fairly strong and durable, but it can also be brittle, it loses strength when wet, and it rots readily. Its most common use as cordage is twine for gardening and package tying. Jute rope is rarely put to heavy-duty use, but it is used decoratively. It is, according to one S&M website, "the traditional choice in rope for bondage."

Coir

Made from the fiber of coconut shells, coir is one of the few natural fiber ropes that will float. It holds knots well, but that's about the sum of its benefits. Coir has poor durability and very high stretch, and is quite coarse. It is the weakest of the natural rope fibers, so ropes tend to be made in large diameters to compensate. Coir rope is rarely found in Western hardware stores or chandleries, but it is available for craft purposes and is still widely used in the production of floor mats.

Ropes made from plant fibers like coir have a natural, rustic appearance

Natural Versus Synthetic Fibers

Synthetic fiber Rope

Most synthetic fibers can be produced in essentially endless lengths. Simply by eliminating the need to overlap short, discontinuous lengths of fiber within the twisted yarns, synthetic fibers produce ropes that are lighter and smaller in diameter than natural fiber ropes for a given strength. And since synthetic fibers are themselves stronger than natural fibers, even lighter weights and smaller diameters can be achieved. In fact, synthetic rope is often two to four times as strong as natural fiber rope of equivalent diameter, while weighing half as much.

Some synthetic ropes float in water and others do not. Some shrink when wet, but most lose little strength, and all are highly resistant to rot. One of the few common drawbacks of synthetics is their slipperiness (especially when wet), which impairs their knot-holding ability. Some synthetics have a natural appearance and color (white, tan, or black), but many are brightly colored, which can be an aid to visibility and identification.

Bright colors can make synthetic ropes easy to identify

Nylon

Nylon (or aliphatic polyamide) was the first synthetic rope fiber, and it is still one of the best and most popular for demanding applications. It is very strong and durable, and it holds knots well, but it does not float in water and it loses a significant amount of strength when wet. Nylon is very stretchy, which is helpful when used as anchor and mooring lines and as dynamic climbing rope, to absorb shock loads in the case of a fall.

Polypropylene

Among the least expensive and weakest of synthetic cordage fibers, polypropylene (also known as polypro or simply "poly") is very light in weight, floating higher in water than polyethylene. It does not shrink when wet, but it is less durable than polyethylene and it degrades quickly with exposure to sunlight, making it inappropriate

for long-term outdoor structures or tying up boats. It melts at such a low temperature that it can be damaged just sitting in a closed car on a hot day. The fiber comes in several forms, each lending different characteristics to rope. Polypropylene monofilaments offer the best wear resistance; multifilaments are softer and hold knots better; staple-spun and fibrillated fibers provide a soft, hairy feel; and split-film fibers are the least expensive.

Part One: Rope and Knot Basics

Polyethylene

Polyethylene rope floats and has good abrasion resistance, making it attractive as a tow line for water skiing, wakeboarding, and similar sports. It is slipperier than polypropylene, does not hold knots well, and melts at a fairly low temperature.

Polyester

Often sold under the trade name Dacron®, polyester is almost as strong as nylon when dry, and stronger when wet. It has good durability and knot-holding ability. Polyester rope has moderate stretch, and some types can be purchased pre-stretched for lower elongation in use. It does not float.

High-tech Fibers

Two more synthetic rope materials bear mention, if only to warn against spending a lot of money on high-tech rope with limited practical applications for outdoor activities. Both aramid (Kevlar® is the best-known brand name) and high-modulus polyethylene (HMPE or HMP, best known as the brands Spectra® and Dyneema®) fibers are extremely strong—some three times stronger than nylon—and both exhibit minimal stretch, but neither can be readily knotted without greatly reducing their strength, so splices and special termination fittings are commonly used. Absent some very compelling reason (HMPE is used in combination with other fibers in some specialized static climbing ropes), these exotic and expensive fibers are best left to high-end sailboat racers.

Synthetic Fiber Ropes Compared

Characteristic	Nylon	Polypropylene	Polyethylene	Polyester	Aramid, HMPE
Strength	Very high	Medium	Low	High	Highest
Stretch	Medium to high	Medium	Very high	Very low	Very low
Knot-holding ability	Medium to high	Medium to high	Low	High	Very low
Texture/feel	Soft, smooth	Slippery, stiff, texture varies	Slippery, stiff	Smooth, not very slippery	Stiff
Floats?	No	Yes	Yes	No	Aramid: no; HMPE: yes
Durability and environmental resistance	High	Low to medium	Medium to high	High	Medium
Price	High	Low	Low	Medium	Highest

Caring for Rope

Every other knot book admonishes the reader to take great care of rope, to keep it clean, protect it from bad influences, and sing it to sleep at night. This attitude assumes that all rope is expensive and will be used in safety-critical ways when, in fact, much of the rope in outdoor use has less lofty purposes. Rigging a tarp, hanging clothes to dry, securing gear in a canoe, and lashing up the frame of an emergency shelter do not require expensive, or even particularly strong, cordage. Some of the cordage you bring into the backcountry can be considered not merely expendable but downright consumable, requiring no special care or protection.

That said, rope that is intended for demanding uses—climbing, sailing, and rescue come quickly to mind—is expensive and does need to be cared for in order to maintain proper safety margins and protect your investment. So the following advice does apply, but some of it only to the good stuff.

• Keep rope clean. Keep it out of the dirt. Grains of dirt and sand will damage fibers in the rope and weaken it. Wash dirty rope.

• Don't step on rope. It tends to grind dirt into the fibers.

• Keep rope away from solvents, petroleum products, and other chemicals.

• Whip, tape, or seal rope ends to prevent fraying. Take these steps before or immediately after cutting a length of rope, and before putting it into use.

• Prevent chafing by avoiding sharp or rough surfaces or by using chafing gear.

• Coil rope neatly and securely before storing or transporting it.

• Store rope away from direct sunlight and excessive heat. Dry wet rope before placing it in storage.

Washing Rope

Rope that's good enough to keep should be washed when it gets dirty. Rope that is used in salt water should be soaked in fresh water at least annually to remove salts, even if it appears clean.

To hand-wash rope, soak it for about 30 minutes in water with liquid dish soap, then use a scrub brush to remove surface dirt. Soak again and rinse to remove the soap, then hang it to dry.

Rope can be machine-washed, but do it separately, not in the same load with your best cocktail dress. Use only a small amount of mild detergent and a small dose of fabric softener. Set the machine to pre-soak for 30 minutes, or do the pre-soak in a bucket before placing the rope in the machine. Top-loading washing machines are your best bet. Some smaller ropes will be okay in a front-loading washing machine, but large heavy ones will drop and pound alarmingly in front-loaders.

Either way you wash the rope, don't dry it in a clothes dryer. Hang it in garlands from a line and allow it to air dry completely before coiling it for storage.

Cutting Rope

Natural fiber ropes must be cut with a knife, while most synthetics can also be melted in two with a heated blade. Almost any folding or fixed-blade knife will do, as long as it has a very sharp plain-edged blade. Serrated blades cut more quickly and are good for emergency and rescue situations, but they leave ragged, frayed ends.

Many stores that sell rope by the foot or the meter off of reels have electric hot-knives (also known as guillotines) to cut synthetic rope, and some allow their customers to use them. (Do not use an electric hot-knife for natural fiber rope.) To use one, turn it on and wait a minute or so for it to reach operating temperature. Press the rope gently and squarely against the blade and the heat will immediately begin melting the fibers. Press slowly so that the fibers are melted together on both sides of the cut. This effectively prevents the rope from fraying. Don't touch the melted ends for several seconds, as they will be hot. Remember to turn the device off when you're done.

Electric hot-knives are not practical for outdoor use, but you can achieve the same results by heating a knife blade until very hot over the flame of a gas camping stove and then immediately applying it to the rope. This is best done with a cheap knife with a long blade, heating it mainly near the tip of the blade. The heat could possibly damage the temper of the blade, so you don't want to use a good knife, and it could damage the handle too, so you don't want to use a knife with a short blade, like most pocket knives.

Preventing Fraying

Never cut a rope without first securing both sides of the cut to prevent unraveling. This applies even to cheap, consumable rope, because a frayed end quickly reduces any rope's usable length and makes it difficult or impossible to work with.

Short of a back splice, which we don't cover, whipping is the only good, nearly permanent method to prevent natural fiber rope unraveling, and a very attractive option for synthetics as well. For whipping instructions, see pp.179–183.

Caring for Rope

When using a cigarette lighter or a match to melt a rope's end, beware of dripping molten plastic onto bare skin or clothing

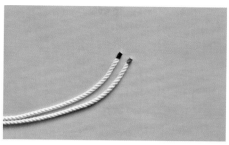

Electrical tape is an effective, if not quite permanent, method to prevent fraying

Melting a rope's end is not pretty, but it's an effective way to prevent fraying

Wrap tape around the rope and cut right through it to secure both new ends against fraying

Melting is an option only for synthetic rope. If the rope is not melt-cut with a heated blade, as described above, the fibers of a cut rope may be melted with a cigarette lighter or other flame (see above). Some synthetic ropes will burn and melt, while others just melt. If the rope catches fire, blow it out before applying the flame again. Beware of dripping the molten plastic onto your skin or clothing.

A melted end will never unravel (although the heat of melting makes the fibers on cheap polypropylene rope so brittle that the end may break off after short usage). On the downside, a melted end is ugly, and it often has

sharp points that inconveniently catch on the rope's fibers when tying knots or coiling. Those points can also occasionally cause skin cuts.

Plastic electrical tape is not as permanent an end-sealer as a whipping, but it works pretty well and is easily replaced. Wrap it two or three times around the rope and cut directly through it, so that both ends are secured in a single operation (see above). For large-diameter rope, cover a longer surface of the rope and make additional wraps.

Dipping a rope's end in carpenter's glue will prevent fraying

Masking tape may be used as a temporary measure only: for example, when cutting lengths at the store, or when cutting just prior to whipping the ends.

Twine or other small stuff can also be used as a strictly temporary measure to prevent fraying. Tie Constrictor Knots (p.151) around the rope on each side of where you will cut. You can't readily tie a knot with a rope whose ends are secured in this manner, but it suffices to keep the ends unfrayed while a whipping is applied.

Rope ends can also be sealed with heat-shrink tubing similar to that used for electrical connections. There are liquid "whipping" solutions into which one dips a rope end. After they dry, these are quite permanent, but they do not work with all types of rope. Dipped finishes can also be applied with polyvinyl acetate (PVA, sold as "white glue" and yellow carpenter's glue) and latex-based glues (see above).

A stopper knot tied in the end of a rope will also prevent fraying. This is often the only practical approach for jute twine or other natural cordage that's too small to whip or tape. It's not a viable permanent solution for good rope, but it has its place as an expedient.

Preventing Chafe

If a rope will move relative to a hard rough surface—in other words, if it will rub—it must be protected from abrasion or chafe. Climbers habitually place chafing gear on top ropes where they pass over sharp rock edges. If specialty gear is not available, a patch of carpeting or a thick piece of cloth will suffice, but it must be secured well to prevent shifting and loss.

Where the same, relatively short section of a rope will be subjected to abrasion repeatedly (as on a dedicated dockline for a boat in its regular berth), then it is often practical to protect only that section with a piece of plastic tubing or hose (see right). This can be held in place attractively with heavy whippings on both ends, or with duct tape if appearance is not a priority. If the rope can't be pushed through a tight-fitting piece of tubing, then the tubing can be split lengthwise and sewn right onto the rope with a heavy-duty sailmaker's needle and palm. A third option, usually employed when the rope will remain stationary and something else will rub against it (usually another rope), is service (p.183): a tight

wrapping of heavy whipping thread around the section of rope in question.

If different ropes will be used regularly against a rough edge that would cause rapid abrasion (as in a canal lock or a gas dock, where different boats are always tying up), then the edge itself may be protected with a patch of leather, a sheet of plastic, or a smoothly curved piece of sheet metal fastened permanently in place (see below).

Plastic hose may be applied to a section of rope that will be frequently subject to abrasion

Alternately, a hard edge can be protected with a sheet of plastic, metal, or leather to prevent chafe

Coiling for Storage

To avoid tangles, rope must be secured in coils for storage and transportation. Coiled ropes are easier to carry and much faster to access and use than tangled ones.

Laid rope coils well in only one direction, and if coiled wrong produces twists and kinks. The vast majority of laid rope has a right-hand twist, known as Z-laid. To determine the lay of a rope, hold a section vertically: if the strands twist upward from left to right, it is Z-laid; if they twist upward from right to left, it is the opposite: a left-hand twist, known as S-laid.

Coil Z-laid rope clockwise and S-laid rope counterclockwise. With each length of rope that you gather into a loop, give it a full 360-degree twist away from you around its own axis before adding it to the coil.

Most braided rope coils equally well in either direction, but should always be coiled in the same direction, as the fibers may take a "set" after lengthy storage and resist being coiled the other way. Some braided ropes, however, have laid cores that want to coil in only one direction (usually clockwise), and others naturally take to being coiled in figure 8s.

Climbing ropes have permanently attached end labels that show their length, and this is a great idea for all stored rope. Add labels or tags that indicate length, along with any other characteristics not

immediately apparent (e.g., fiber type, working load, previous use), to your stored ropes so that you can reliably select the right one for the job without having to uncoil and measure it.

In addition to the coiling methods on the following pages, one more simple method of securing a coil bears mention: stopping it. To stop a coil, use short lengths of twine or other small stuff; make two round

turns around the coil near one of the rope's ends (or around both ends if they overlap near each other on the circumference of the coil). Tie the small stuff with a Slipped Square Knot (p.77), Constrictor Knot (p.151), or Packer's Knot (p.84). Tie similar knots at a minimum of two (preferably three) other points equally spaced on the circumference of the coil.

Alpine Coil

Also known as: Mountaineer's Coil, Climber's Coil, Lap Coil, Standing Coil

This method of coiling is quick and easy, and it works for short as well as long lengths of rope. If made large enough, the finished coil can be carried slung diagonally across the chest and can be uncoiled with the standing part still attached to one's climbing harness. But because it secures the coils at only one point on the circumference, it is somewhat prone to tangles.

Uses: storing and transporting long or short lengths of rope

Pros: quick and easy to make and release

Cons: tangles more readily than Wrapped and Reef-knotted and Butterfly Coils

Instructions

1. Coil the rope, leaving a couple of feet (60 cm) loose at both ends (less for a small coil). For a long length of rope, each coil can be the length of both arms stretched out. Form a bight in the standing end.

2. Bring the working end to the inside of the coil.

3. Wrap the working end around the coils, capturing both parts of the bight against the coils with a Single Hitch (p.54).

Alpine Coil

4. Make at least three round turns around the bight and the coils, then pass the working end through the bight.

5. Ready to tighten.

Untying: Pull the bight back through the round turns to loosen the working end.

6. Pull the free end of the bight so that the bight captures the working end.

7. The completed Alpine Coil.

Fireman's Coil

This is one of the quickest and easiest coils to make. It's not so well suited for transporting rope, but its built-in hanging loop makes it ideal for storing it. However, it may not hold in slippery synthetic stuff.

Uses: storing long or short lengths of rope

Pros: quick and easy, has hanging loop, releases instantly

Cons: tangles more readily than Wrapped and Reef-knotted and Butterfly Coils; not as secure as Alpine Coil

Instructions

1. Coil the rope, leaving 2–3 ft. (70–100 cm) loose at the working end. Form an overhand crossing turn in the working part where it leaves the last coil, and make a bight closer to the working end.

2. Pass the bight through the coil so that it is on the opposite side from the crossing turn.

3. Pass the bight through the crossing turn from back to front.

4. Pull the bight so that the crossing turn closes tightly around it.

5. The finished coil.

Untying: Pull the working end so that the hanging loop comes through the crossing turn.

Wrapped and Reef-knotted Coil

Also known as: Wrapped Coil, Wrapped Square-knotted Coil

Unlike the Alpine and Fireman's Coils (p.38, p.40), which secure the coils at only one point on their circumference, this method secures the coils all the way around. This is time-consuming to do, and it makes the rope less available for ready use. But it is an effective method of preventing tangles in rope that will be stored for long periods or transported with other gear in a car trunk or boat locker.

Uses: storing and transporting long lengths of rope

Pros: very secure; effectively prevents tangles

Cons: time-consuming to make and unmake

Instructions

1. Coil the rope, leaving about 3 ft. (100 cm) loose at both ends.

2. Tie a Half Knot (p.55) with the two ends.

3. Tie another Half Knot in the opposite direction, completing a Square Knot (p.76).

Untying: Untie the second Square Knot, unwrap the spiral wraps, then untie the first Square Knot.

Wrapped and Reef-knotted Coil

4. Begin wrapping one end in spirals around the coils, making each wrap 2–3 in. (5–8 cm) from the previous one. Continue wrapping until it is opposite from the Square Knot.

5. Begin wrapping the other end in identical spirals around the other side of the coil. These wraps should *not* be a mirror image of the first set. They should continue the spiral direction of the first set of wraps.

6. Continue the second wrap until it is opposite the Square Knot.

7. Tie a Half Knot with the ends.

8. Tie a second Half Knot in the opposite direction, to complete a second Square Knot.

9. The completed coil.

Butterfly Coil

Also known as: Backpack Coil, Backpacker's Coil

A climbing rope of 200 ft. (60 m) or more makes a bulky, heavy load to carry, and a time-consuming mess if tangled during transportation. The weight of the Butterfly Coil is carried on both shoulders like a backpack, and the coil is secured around the waist, which prevents it from swinging and catching while climbing. But unlike the Alpine Coil (p.38), it must be removed and undone before it can be attached to a climbing harness.

Uses: carrying climbing rope

Pros: secure, comfortable

Cons: interferes with carrying a real backpack; must be undone to attach rope to climbing harness

Instructions

1. Working on clean ground, double the rope by bringing both ends together and pulling both parts equally through one hand. The rope should be laid out before you with no tangles or kinks.

2. Pull about 20 ft. (6 m) of rope into the ends, then place both parts over your shoulders and behind your neck. (The ends are out of frame to the left side of the photograph, i.e., to the climber's right.) For brevity, we'll call the long, doubled rope on the side opposite the ends the "standing part."

3. Pull an arm's length of the standing part, forming the first "butterfly wing" (on the right side of the photograph). Bring your arm all the way down to draw the greatest length possible into this wing.

4. Pull another arm's length of the standing part with the other arm and place it behind your neck.

Untying: Untie the Square Knot that secures the coil around your waist. Unwrap the ends from your waist, remove from over your shoulders, extract the ends from the bight, unwrap the round turns, and unfold the coils so they lay full-length on the ground.

Butterfly Coil

5. Bring that arm down all the way, forming the second butterfly wing (on the left side of the photograph).

6. Switching to the other arm again, pull another arm's length of the standing part behind your neck and bring it down to your side.

7. Continue pulling loops into the doubled rope and placing them over your neck on alternating sides until all of the standing part is over your shoulders.

8. Remove the coil from your neck, supporting its folded shape over the arm opposite from the working ends.

9. Wrap the working ends around the folded coil just below the supporting arm, leaving enough room to remove your hand.

10. Continue wrapping the working ends downward over the coil until about 10 ft. (3 m) of both ends remain.

Butterfly Coil

11. Make a bight in the working ends about 1 ft (30 cm) from the last wrap.

12. Pass the bight to the hand that supports the coil, then pull that hand through the top of the coil, pulling the bight through as well.

13. Pull the working ends all the way through the bight, so that they support the coil.

14. Holding one working end in each hand, hoist the coil high onto your back.

15. Bring the working ends down over your shoulders like backpack shoulder straps. Take both hands behind your back and switch the ends of the rope between your hands. Bring your arms out to the side so that the crossed ends secure the coil against your back.

16. Bring your arms to the front and tie the rope ends together around your waist with a Square Knot (p.76) or a Double Slipped Square Knot as shown (see Slipped Square Knot, p.77).

Part Two
Foundation Knots

Most knots, bends, and hitches incorporate simpler structures which are themselves knots. The knots in this section are all easy to learn and tie. Some of them are useful in their own right, while all of them are important as components of more complex knots or for understanding basic procedures or principles that come into play when tying them.

1. Overhand Knot

Uses: stopper, binding, hand grips, to prevent fraying

Pros: quick, easy; forms the basis of many other knots

Cons: difficult to untie; not secure

Page: 48

2. Slipped Overhand Knot

Uses: stopper, simple noose

Pros: quick and easy to tie and release; larger than Overhand Knot

Cons: less secure than a standard Overhand Knot

Page: 49

3. Double Overhand Knot

Uses: stopper, binding, handholds

Pros: quick and easy to tie; more secure than Overhand Knot

Cons: hard to untie

Page: 51

4. Overhand Loop

Uses: fixed loop anywhere on a rope; attachment, tie-off, or purchase point

Pros: quick and easy to tie even if neither end is free

Cons: difficult to untie

Page: 53

5. Single Hitch

Uses: hitch to maintain light, instantly released tension; hold an end in place temporarily

Pros: ties and releases instantly

Cons: extremely insecure

Page: 54

6. Half Knot

Uses: light-duty or temporary binding of bundles or packages

Pros: quick and easy to tie; easily untied

Cons: insecure

Page: 55

7. Half Hitch

Uses: maintain light tension on an object that must be easily released

Pros: quick and easy to tie and untie

Cons: insecure; slips easily

Page: 56

8. Slipped Half Hitch

Uses: maintain light tension on an object that must be easily released

Pros: easy to tie, quicker to release than Half Hitch

Cons: insecure; slips easily

Page: 57

1. Overhand Knot

Also known as: Simple Knot, Thumb Knot

The Overhand Knot is the most basic "true knot," in which the rope is tied to itself. In spite of its simplicity, it is useful in its own right and of paramount importance as the foundation of many other knots. And in spite of its name, it can be tied either overhand or underhand.

Uses: stopper, binding, creating a series of handholds along a length of line; preventing fraying at the end of a line

Pros: quick and easy to tie; forms the basis of many other knots

Cons: difficult to untie if tightened hard; can slip; not secure as a binding

Instructions

1. Make an overhand crossing turn.

2. Pass the working end under the standing part.

3. Pull the working end through the crossing turn.

4. Pull both ends to tighten.

Untying: Grab the standing part where it crosses the working part, and the working part where it crosses the standing part, and pull in opposite directions. If it is tied very tight in twisted line, it can be helpful to twist the working end with the lay of the rope and push it under the crossing. In extreme cases, a fid might be needed to loosen the knot.

2. **Slipped Overhand Knot**

Also known as: Slip Knot, Running Knot, Overhand Knot with Drawloop

Many knots can be tied "slipped," or with a drawloop, in which the working end is formed into a bight before it is captured by another part of the knot. Never use the bight in the working end of a slipped knot as a loop to bear a load: it will not hold. But if the working end of the Slipped Overhand Knot is left extra long, it can be turned around so that the working end serves as the standing part, and the drawloop can then function as a simple noose.

Uses: stopper, simple noose

Pros: quick and easy to tie and release; bulkier than a standard Overhand Knot

Cons: less secure than a standard Overhand Knot; not as effective as some other stopper knots

Instructions

1. Make an overhand crossing turn.

2. Form a bight in the working end.

3. Pass the bight under the standing part and partway through the crossing turn.

2. Slipped Overhand Knot

Untying: Grab the working end and pull. It may get harder when the end of the bight reaches the crossing turn, but more effort will usually succeed in pulling it through, unless the rope is so stiff that it won't take a tight radius.

4. The knot before tightening.

5. To tighten, pull the standing part with one hand, and the bight with the other hand. Be careful not to draw the working end through the crossing turn when tightening or you'll be left with a standard Overhand Knot (p.48).

3. **Double Overhand Knot**

Also known as: Doubled Thumb or Simple Knot

"Doubling" (taking part of the rope and passing it through a crossing turn or other element twice) is another basic procedure used in many knots. Doubling creates more bulk and increases friction, which equates to holding power. While the Double Overhand Knot is larger overall than a standard Overhand Knot (p.48), its diameter is the same so it won't prevent the rope from running through a larger hole.

Uses: stopper, binding, handholds along a line

Pros: quick and easy to tie; less likely to slip than a standard Overhand Knot

Cons: hard to untie if tightened hard

Instructions

1. Make an Overhand Knot (p.48)

2. Pass the working end through the crossing turn a second time.

Untying: Use your thumbs to pry apart the two adjacent crossing turns on either side of the knot, then pull the working end through the crossing turn in the standing part

3. The "doubled" aspect of this knot is clear before you tighten it.

3. Double Overhand Knot

4. As you pull both ends, the knot changes form.

5. Work the knot into shape by pushing it up from the standing part toward the working end.

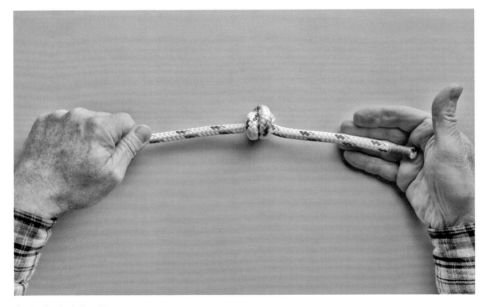

6. The finished, faired knot.

4. Overhand Loop

Also known as: Loop Knot

The Overhand Loop is simply an Overhand Knot (p.48) tied in a bight. Among the simplest of loops, it is fixed (i.e., non-adjustable) and, if placed under much strain, it becomes so tight that it should be considered untieable.

Uses: forming a fixed loop anywhere along the length of a rope or at the end; useful as a handhold, an attachment point for hardware, a loop from which to hang objects, and a purchase through which a working end can be passed in order to pull the standing part tight

Pros: quick and easy to tie even if neither end is free

Cons: very difficult to untie if tightened hard

Instructions

1. Form a bight near the working end or anywhere along the rope.

2. Make a crossing turn with the bight across both the standing part and the working end.

3. Pass the bight through the crossing turn.

4. Holding the standing part and working end together in one hand, pull the bight to tighten.

Untying: Grab either strand of the bight just before it passes under the standing parts, and either strand of the standing part where it passes over the bight, and pull in opposite directions. Generally, however, you should consider this knot to be permanent and be prepared to cut it.

5. Single Hitch

Also known as: Half Knot

Almost too rudimentary to be considered a knot, the Single Hitch is just a crossing turn around an object. It will hold given perfect conditions of friction, angle, and load, but even then with only minimal security. Of limited use by itself, it serves as an element of many other knots.

Uses: as a hitch to maintain light tension on an object that must be instantly releasable; as an element of other knots, to hold one end in place pending a subsequent procedure

Pros: quick and easy; can be released instantly

Cons: extremely insecure

Instructions

1. There's scarcely anything to a Single Hitch. Take a crossing turn around an object and capture the working end against it with the standing part, or vice versa.

Untying: Release tension and the structure simply falls apart.

6. Half Knot

Also known as: Overhand Knot

Even if they don't know it by name, everyone knows the Half Knot as the first step in tying a shoelace. It is the simplest of binding knots and forms the foundation for many important and more secure bindings and bends. When tied in a single piece of cordage, it's just an Overhand Knot (p.48) tied around an object. But it may also be tied in the working ends of two different cords.

Uses: light-duty or temporary binding of bundles or packages

Pros: quick and easy to tie; easily untied

Cons: insecure

Instructions

1. Cross one end over the other.

2. Take either end and tuck it under the opposite one.

3. Pull both working ends to tighten.

4. The Half Knot may be tied with the ends of two ropes.

Untying: Pull the standing parts in opposite directions.

7. Half Hitch

Also known as: Single Hitch

The Half Hitch is much like the Overhand Knot (p.48) or Half Knot (p.55), but the working end doubles back on itself to form a crossing turn around the standing part. An essential component of innumerable other knots, it is of limited usefulness by itself because it is not secure.

Uses: to pull or maintain light tension on an object that must be easily released

Pros: quick and easy to tie; more secure than a Single Hitch

Cons: insecure; slips easily; holds only with light constant tension at certain angles

Instructions

Untying: Pull a little slack into the standing part, then pull the working end through the crossing turn that surrounds the object.

1. Take a turn around an object and cross the working end over the standing part.

2. Pass the working end through the crossing turn from back to front.

4. The finished Half Hitch.

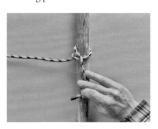

3. While maintaining tension on the standing part, pull the working end tight so that it forms an overhand crossing turn around the standing part and lies perpendicular to it.

8. Slipped Half Hitch

Also known as: Half Hitch with a Drawloop

Tie a Slipped Overhand Knot (p.49) around an object and you've got a Slipped Half Hitch. It has the same benefits and disadvantages as a regular Half Hitch (p.56) but the drawloop makes it even easier to untie.

Uses: to maintain light tension on an object that must be easily released

Pros: quick and easy to tie; more easily released than a regular Half Hitch

Cons: insecure; slips easily; holds only with light constant tension

Instructions

1. Make a crossing turn around an object and form the working end into a bight.

2. Pull the bight partway through the crossing turn.

3. Pull the bight and the standing part to tighten, being careful not to pull the working end through the crossing turn.

Untying: Just pull the working end and the knot will fall open.

Part Three
Stopper Knots

Stopper knots are "true knots"—structures tied within the rope itself and not to anything else. Most often tied at the end of a rope, stopper knots get their name from their common function of stopping a rope from running out through a small opening through which they pass, such as a pulley block, a fairlead on a boat, or a grommet on a tarp. Other common uses are to form "knobs" on the rope that can be easily held or pulled, or to add weight to the end so that it can be thrown.

9. & 10. Figure 8 Knot

Uses: stopper for sailboat sheets, fender pennants, tarp guylines; handhold

Pros: quick and easy to tie and untie; reduction of rope strength is small

Cons: will not stop a hole larger than Overhand Knot

Pages: 60, 61 (alternate method)

11. Slipped Figure 8 Knot

Uses: stopper that can be quickly untied to pull through an opening

Pros: quick and easy to tie; nearly instantaneous to untie

Cons: will not stop a larger hole than Overhand Knot

Page: 62

12. Stopper Knot

Uses: stopper, handhold, heaving line

Pros: large, comfortable, attractive; easy to tie

Cons: only good for medium diameter rope; smaller and lighter than a Heaving Line Knot; can create kinks

Page: 63

13. Sink Stopper Knot

Uses: stopper, especially in thinner rope

Pros: stops larger holes than many other stopper knots

Cons: very difficult to untie

Page: 65

14. Stevedore Knot

Uses: stopper

Pros: large; easy to untie

Cons: smaller than a Sink Stopper

Page: 67

15. Heaving Line Knot

Uses: add weight to the end of a heaving line

Pros: adjustable for size and weight; works with any size cordage

Cons: time-consuming

Page: 69

16. Monkey's Fist

Uses: add weight to the end of a heaving line; decorative pulls

Pros: easily thrown; weight adjustable with different cores

Cons: complicated and time-consuming

Page: 71

9. Figure 8 Knot

Also known as: Figure of 8 Knot, Flemish Knot

One of the most common and most useful stopper knots, the Figure 8 is simple to tie and remember. It is frequently used to prevent lines from running through small openings, and though it is not much bigger than an Overhand Knot, it is easily untied. It is the basis for a whole family of related knots.

Uses: stopper, sailboat main and jib sheets, fender pennants, tarp guylines

Pros: quick and easy to tie and untie; provides a good size handhold at a rope's end

Cons: will not stop a hole larger than an Overhand Knot

Instructions

1. Make an overhand crossing turn, then pass the working end back under the standing part.

2. Bring the working end forward and over the upper strand of the crossing turn.

3. Pass the working end through the crossing turn.

4. Pull both ends to tighten.

Untying: Grab the tops of the two crossing turns. Pull the working end through the turn on the standing end.

10. **Figure 8 Knot**—Alternate Method

Also known as: Figure of 8 Knot, Flemish Knot

This is simply a different way to manipulate the rope when tying the Figure 8 Knot (opposite). The finished knots are identical. You may or may not find it easier to use, but it's included to illustrate how different knotting procedures can achieve the same ends.

Uses: stopper, sailboat main and jib sheets, fender pennants, tarp guylines

Pros: quick and easy to tie and untie; provides a good size handhold at a rope's end

Cons: will not stop a hole larger than an Overhand Knot

Instructions

Untying: Grab the tops of the two crossing turns. Pull the working end through the turn on the standing end.

1. Make a bight near the working end of the rope. Grab the end of the bight and begin to twist it around the standing part.

2. Continue twisting so that the working end crosses over the standing part.

3. Continue twisting. A second crossing turn will begin to form.

4. After twisting the bight a full 360 degrees, the working end crosses under and over the standing part.

5. Pass the working end through the first crossing turn (i.e., the bight) from back to front. Pull both ends to tighten.

11. Slipped Figure 8 Knot

Also known as: Figure of 8 Knot or Flemish Knot with a Drawloop

As easy as it may be to untie a Figure 8 Knot (p.60), placing a drawloop in the working end to "slip" it makes it easier and quicker still.

Uses: stopper that can be quickly untied to pull through an opening

Pros: quick and easy to tie; nearly instantaneous to untie

Cons: will not stop a hole larger than an Overhand Knot

Instructions

1. Make an overhand crossing turn, pass the working end back under the standing part, and form a bight in the working end.

2. Bring the bight forward and partway through the crossing turn from front to back.

3. Pull the bight and the standing part, being careful not to pull the working end through the first crossing turn.

Untying: Pull the working end to bring the bight through the crossing turn.

4. Continue pulling the bight and the standing part to tighten.

12. **Stopper Knot**

This specific stopper knot is named the Stopper Knot. It will stop a hole bigger than an Overhand or Figure 8 Knot (p.48, p.60), makes an attractive and comfortable "handle" at the end of a rope, and adds enough weight so that the end of the rope can be thrown.

Uses: stopper, handhold, heaving line

Pros: large, comfortable, attractive; easy to tie

Cons: only works well in rope of medium diameters; more time-consuming than other stopper knots; cannot be made as large or heavy as the Heaving Line Knot; kinks can make it awkward to untie

Instructions

1. Form a bight around one or two fingers, leaving a long working end.

2. Bring the working end over the standing part, forming a crossing turn around your fingers.

3. Continue wrapping the working end around your fingers, working toward the standing part. Make at least five round turns.

4. Slip the coil onto the fingers of your opposite hand, being careful that it doesn't fall apart. Take a final turn with the working end around the standing part, then pass it up through the coil along your restraining fingers.

12. **Stopper Knot**

Untying: Bend the knot back and forth to separate the turns. Bend the first (crossing) turn down far enough to pull the working end through. Bend each round turn down in turn and pull the working end through until you can pull it out of the bottom of the knot.

5. Pull the working end through.

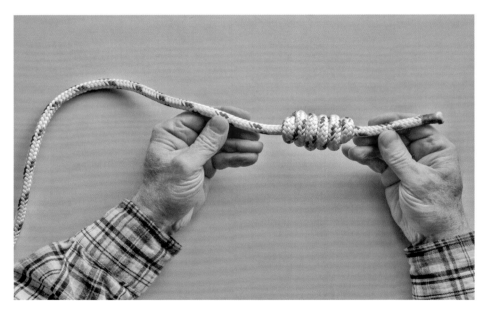

6. Pull both ends. The round turns will need to be worked into shape for a faired knot.

13. **Sink Stopper Knot**

This stopper knot is larger than Overhand or Figure 8 Knots (p.48, p.60) and will stop a rope through a significantly larger hole, but it's shorter and less obtrusive than the Stopper Knot (p.63).

Uses: stopper, especially in thinner rope
Pros: stops holes larger than many other stopper knots
Cons: very difficult to untie if tightened hard

Instructions

1. Make a counterclockwise overhand crossing turn. Form a bight in the standing part.

2. Pass the bight into the top of the crossing turn.

3. Pull the bight through to form a Slipped Overhand Knot (p.49).

4. Pass the working end across the front of the standing part and through the back of the drawloop.

13. Sink Stopper Knot

5. Pull both ends to tighten.

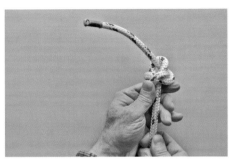

6. Push the knot up from the standing part to fair it.

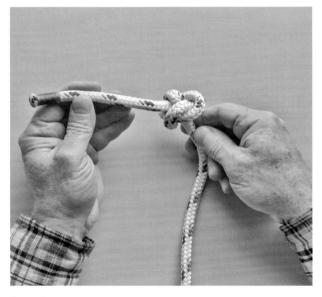

7. The finished knot.

Untying: The Sink Stopper is difficult to untie and may have to be cut. Sometimes, though, it can be untied by creating little bits of slack in small stages. Pull alternately on: i) the opposite sides of the crossing turn; ii) one side of the crossing turn and the working end just before it passes through the bight; and iii) the other side of the crossing turn and the working end before it passes through the bight. Eventually, you may gain enough slack to release the working end from the bight.

14. Stevedore Knot

Also known as: Stevedore's Knot

Before cargo was shipped in containers, stevedores unloaded ships with a block and tackle. If the end of a rope slipped through a pulley block, precious time was lost and cargo could come crashing down—hence the need for an effective stopper knot. The Stevedore Knot will stop a hole larger than a Figure 8 Knot (p.60) but not as large as a Sink Stopper Knot (p.65).

Uses: stopper
Pros: large; easy to untie
Cons: smaller than a Sink Stopper

Instructions

1. Make a clockwise overhand crossing turn and pass the working end back under the standing part, like the first steps in a Figure 8 Knot (p.60).

2. Wrap the working end in a round turn around the standing part.

3. Bring the working end forward and pass it through the top of the crossing turn.

4. Pull both ends to begin tightening.

14. **Stevedore Knot**

Untying: Grab the crossing turn in one hand and the two round turns in the other. Pull the standing part through the round turns to free the working end.

5. Push the knot up from the standing part to fair it.

6. The finished knot.

15. Heaving Line Knot

Also known as: Franciscan Knot

With numerous round turns, the Heaving Line Knot is reminiscent of the Stopper Knot (p.63). Both can add weight to the end of a rope so that it can be thrown, but the methods of tying are different, and the Heaving Line Knot can be made much larger by adding round turns. It can be made wider as well, by adding two or four additional, slightly shorter bights before beginning the round turns.

Uses: heaving line
Pros: adjustable for length and thickness; works with any weight cordage
Cons: time-consuming

Instructions

1. Make a clockwise overhand crossing turn and pass the working end back under both strands of the turn.

2. Begin wrapping the working end up toward the bight that is formed.

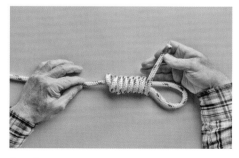

3. Make as many round turns around the bight as the working end allows while leaving a few inches to work with.

4. Pass the working end through the bight.

15. **Heaving Line Knot**

5. Holding the working end against the last round turn, begin pulling the standing part through the coil.

6. Keep pulling until the bight tightens over the working end, locking it in place.

7. The finished knot.

Untying: Flex the knot from side to side, then pull the bight until it releases the working end.

16. Monkey's Fist

This practical, nearly spherical heaving line knot is so attractive that some folks make tiny decorative versions as key fobs or zipper pulls. It's designed to hold a weight in its core so that it can be thrown farther, but it uses enough rope so that it works pretty well even with lightweight cores like a ball of aluminum foil. For more weight, use a round stone, a wooden sphere, or a steel ball, but be careful not to hit the recipient with such a heavy knot.

Uses: heaving line; decorative knobs and pulls

Pros: easily thrown; weight adjustable with different cores

Cons: complicated and time-consuming to tie and untie

Instructions

1. Leaving a long working end, make three round turns around your non-dominant hand, working from the wrist toward the fingertips.

2. Pass the working end around the back of the round turns.

Using a Heaving Line
To throw a heavy rope across a wide gap, tie the monkey's fist in medium-weight rope to make a size convenient for throwing, leaving a relatively short standing part. Tie the standing part to a lightweight "messenger line" longer than the gap, and tie the other end of the messenger line to the heavy rope. The person on the other end of the gap who receives your toss will use the messenger line to pull the heavier line across.

3. Make three round turns at right angles to the first set of round turns, working from bottom to top.

4. Pass the working end through the first set of round turns from front to back.

5. The working end will now encircle the strands on one side of the first set of round turns, above the second set of round turns. Don't pull it tight! The round turns must remain parallel to one another.

6. Working inside the first set of round turns, pass the working end under the second set of round turns from back to front, and then bring it over the second set of round turns from front to back.

7. Make three round turns around the second set of round turns and inside the first set of round turns, keeping everything fairly loose.

8. Place a sphere into the hollow center of the knot.

9. Tuck the bitter end under the first set of round turns. (Alternately, leave a long working end and seize it to the standing part when the knot is complete. See Seizing, page 179.)

16. **Monkey's Fist**

Untying: Untying is the opposite of tying. Free the working end and pull it all the way through each round turn, one turn at a time.

10. Keeping the bitter end in place, tighten the knot by pulling out the slack one round turn at a time, starting at the bitter end and working all the way back to the standing part.

11. The finished Monkey's Fist.

Part Four
Binding Knots

Binding knots are tied tightly around an object or objects, either to secure the object itself (as when tying up a package or bundle), or to anchor one end of the rope solidly to an object as a first step in making a solid connection with another object—for example, when lashing two poles together to build a shelter (see Lashings, pp.160–169).

17. Square Knot

Uses: packages, bundles, reefing sails, bending ropes end-to-end

Pros: simple to tie and untie; fairly secure

Cons: can slip; works as a bend only with ropes of equal diameter; difficult to untie under load; difficult to make tight as a binding

Page: 76

18. Slipped Sqaure Knot

Uses: packages and bundles that must be untied easily; bootlaces

Pros: easy to tie; secure under load; unties easily

Cons: not very secure if not under load

Page: 77

19. Granny Knot

Uses: object lesson in improper knotting

Pros: none

Cons: unstable; slips easily

Page: 78

20. Thief Knot

Uses: binding packages or sacks

Pros: fairly secure; signals pilferage

Cons: can't be tied tightly

Page: 79

21. Surgeon's Knot

Uses: packages, bundles, surgical ligatures

Pros: secure, resists slipping, easier to tie tight under load than a Square Knot

Cons: requires more force than a Square Knot to tighten; more difficult to untie

Page: 80

22. Surgeon's Knot with Second Tuck

Uses: packages, bundles, slippery items

Pros: more secure than a regular Surgeon's Knot, good for slippery rope

Cons: more difficult to untie than a regular Surgeon's Knot

Page: 81

23. Strangle Knot

Uses: temporary rope whipping, bag closure, general-purpose hitch

Pros: fairly secure; easy to tie

Cons: less secure than Constrictor Knot; difficult to untie

Page: 82

24. Miller's Knot

Uses: bag closure

Pros: secure; easy to tie with one or both hands

Cons: not as secure as a Constrictor Knot; can be difficult to untie

Page: 83

25. Packer's Knot

Uses: packages, bundles

Pros: adjustable for tightness; works in thin or medium cordage

Cons: more complex than a Square or Surgeon's Knot

Page: 84

17. Square Knot

Also known as: Reef Knot, Hercules Knot

Composed of one Half Knot (p.55) on top of another, the Square Knot is supremely useful both as a binding knot (when tying the rope to itself around another object), and as a bend (to tie the ends of two ropes together). A good mnemonic for tying it correctly is "right over left; left over right." It can be readily reversed, tying it "left over right; right over left."

Uses: packages, bundles, reefing sails; bending ropes end-to-end

Pros: simple to tie and untie; fairly secure

Cons: can slip; works as a bend only with ropes of equal diameter; difficult to untie if under load; difficult to tighten as a binding

Instructions

1. Make a Half Knot (p.55) with the right working end over then under the left working end.

2. Bend both working ends back toward their own standing parts. Take the working end that is now on the left and pass it over the one that is now on the right.

3. Pass the first working end through the bight that has formed in the other rope, from back to front. You've just made a second Half Knot in the opposite direction. Pull both working ends tight.

4. Pull both standing parts tight.

Untying: Pull the working-end sides of the bights in opposite directions.

18. **Slipped Square Knot**

Also known as: Reef Knot or Hercules Knot with a Drawloop

A single drawloop makes this simple variation of the Square Knot (opposite) easy to untie, even under tension. You probably know another variation, called a Double Slipped Square Knot, in which drawloops are added to both ends: it's how you tie your shoes.

Uses: packages and bundles that must be tied securely and untied easily; bootlaces (when tied with two drawloops)

Pros: easy to tie and remember; secure under load, unties easily

Cons: not very secure if not under load

Instructions (NB R1 = Rope 1, R2 = Rope 2)

Untying: Pull the working end to draw the bight through the loop of the standing part.

1. Make a Half Knot (p.55), placing the working end of the rope to the right (henceforth, R1) over, then under, the working end of the rope to the left (henceforth, R2), as if you are about to tie a Square Knot (opposite).

2. Make a bight in the working end of R2. Cross the working end of R1 over the working end of the bight.

3. Make a bight in the working end of R1. Reach through the front of the bight in R2 to grab it.

4. Pull the new bight through the first bight from back to front.

5. Tighten by pulling the second bight in one hand and the opposite working end in the other.

19. Granny Knot

Also known as: Lubber's Knot, False Knot, Calf Knot, Booby Knot

A Granny Knot is an incorrectly tied Square Knot (p.76). While it will hold in some noncritical applications, there is never a good reason to use it, as it takes exactly as long to tie, and uses exactly the same amount of rope, as a Square Knot, while offering no advantages whatsoever. It's included here simply to show how not to tie a Square Knot.

Uses: none
Pros: none
Cons: unstable; slips easily

Instructions

1. Pass the right working end over then under the left working end, making a Half Knot (p.55).

2. Instead of "right over left; left over right," as you would for a Square Knot (p.76), pass the new right working end over the new left working end. (Right over left; right over left.)

Untying: Pull the working ends through the bights.

3. Pull each working end through the bight made by the other end. Hold the working and standing parts of one rope together in each hand, and pull to tighten.

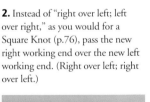

4. The right working end passes first over, then under the bight of the left working end, and vice versa. In a Square Knot, in comparison, one end crosses the bight above-and-above, while the other crosses below-and-below.

5. Pulled tight, the Granny Knot collapses. Pulled even tighter, it will probably slip.

20. Thief Knot

Also known as: Bag Knot, Bread Bag Knot

The Thief Knot is designed to resemble the Square Knot (p.76). The idea is that a thief who steals something from a sack of provisions will retie a proper Square Knot to cover his tracks, but the owner will notice the difference. (Of course, the missing provisions will also tip off the owner, but that's folk wisdom for you.)

Uses: binding packages or sacks while supposedly signaling pilferage

Pros: fairly secure

Cons: can't be tied tightly

Instructions

1. Imagine that we have made a tight round turn around the neck of a sack out of the frame at the top of the photo. Make a bight in the left end of the rope. Pass the other end through the bight from back to front.

2. Pass the working end around the bight, going first over the working end of the bight, next around the back of the bight, then forward.

3. Pass the working end through the bight from front to back. Pull both working ends, then the standing parts tight.

Untying: Pull the working-end sides of the bights in opposite directions.

4. The finished knot has some of the Square Knot's symmetry, in that both strands of the right end of the rope pass under the bight of the left end, and both strands of the left end of the rope pass over the bight of the right end. But where both working ends are on the same side of a Square Knot, the working ends are on opposite sides of the Thief Knot—a subtle difference.

21. Surgeon's Knot

Also known as: Ligature Knot

Another variation of the Square Knot (p.76), this one holds better and is easier to tie tightly as a binding knot. The second tuck provides extra friction, holding the structure tight until the knot is finished. Surgeons used this knot to tie off slippery blood vessels.

Uses: packages, bundles, surgical ligatures

Pros: secure; resists slipping; easier to tie tight under load than a Square Knot

Cons: requires more muscle than a Square Knot to tighten; more difficult to untie

Instructions

1. Start as if you are tying a Square Knot around an object, but tuck the right working end over and under the left working end a second time before pulling tight.

2. Bring the working end that is now on the left and pass it over and under the other working end, like finishing a Square Knot. Pull tight.

Untying: Free both working ends by simultaneously pulling them through the bights.

3. The finished Surgeon's Knot looks like what it is: a Square Knot with an extra tuck.

22. Surgeon's Knot with Second Tuck

Also known as: Doubled Surgeon's Knot

This variation of the Surgeon's Knot adds a second tuck to the top Half Knot (p.55) for extra security.

Uses: packages, bundles, slippery items

Pros: more secure than a regular Surgeon's Knot; helpful when using slippery rope

Cons: more difficult to untie than a regular Surgeon's Knot

Instructions

1. Start by tying a Surgeon's Knot (opposite), but don't pull it tight yet.

2. Take one of the working ends and tuck it through the bight in the other end a second time.

3. Pull both working ends to tighten.

Untying: Free both working ends by simultaneously pulling them through the bights. It may be helpful to first untuck the working ends from their second tucks.

23. **Strangle Knot**

Also known as: Double Overhand Knot

The Strangle Knot is often tied with small-diameter stuff around a large-diameter rope that is about to be cut, to hold the strands in place until permanent whipping can be applied. It can also serve as a bag closure and as a more secure alternative to a Clove Hitch (p.149). For even greater tenacity, however, use a Constrictor Knot (p.151).

Uses: temporary rope whipping, bag closure, general-purpose hitch

Pros: fairly secure; easy to tie

Cons: less secure than Constrictor Knot; difficult to untie

Instructions

1. Tie a Double Overhand Knot (p.51) around the object being "strangled." Or you may tie the knot in hand, making the crossing turn large enough to then slip over one end of the object when it's ready.

2. Pull both ends tight.

Untying: This knot can be very difficult to untie. If a fid is not available to work the knot loose, cutting may be the only option.

3. The finished Strangle Knot.

24. Miller's Knot

Also known as: Sack Knot, Bag Knot

This is a good knot to close the top of a sack. It tightens down well and holds securely against a high-friction surface like a canvas or burlap bag. It may be tied with a drawloop to make it easier to untie.

Uses: bag closure

Pros: secure; easy to tie with one or both hands

Cons: not as secure as a Constrictor Knot, but can be difficult to untie nonetheless

Instructions

Untying: Pry the turns away from each other (i.e., toward the top and bottom of the bag) until there is sufficient slack to release the working end.

1. Make a Single Hitch (p.54) around the neck of the bag, holding the standing part down with the longer working end.

2. Bring the working end around the bag to make a round turn over the standing part.

3. Pass the working end over the round turn and through the Single Hitch.

4. Pull both ends to tighten.

5. To form a drawloop that will make the knot easier to untie: at step 3 make the working end into a bight before passing it over the round turn and through the Single Hitch.

25. Packer's Knot

When butchers used to wrap orders in paper, they would tie this knot in string to secure the packages. The standing part can be snugged up as tight as you wish through the Figure 8 Knot (p.60) in the working end.

Uses: packages, bundles

Pros: adjustable for tightness; works well in thin or medium cordage

Cons: more complex than a Square or Surgeon's Knot

Instructions

1. Bring the rope or string around the package and cross the ends as shown. We will refer to the end on the right side of the photograph as the working end.

2. With the working end, make an underhand crossing turn counterclockwise around the standing part. Note how the standing part passes through the crossing turn from front to back.

3. Bring the working end to the front, and pass it through the crossing turn from front to back, over the standing part. You are tying an Overhand Knot (p.48) around the standing part.

4. Pull the Overhand Knot tight.

5. Pull the standing part through the Overhand Knot to tighten the rope around the package.

6. Pass the working end behind the standing part.

7. Pass the working end under itself to complete a Half Hitch (p.56) around the standing part. Pull the Half Hitch tight.

8. The finished Packer's Knot.

Untying: Untie the final Overhand Knot, then pull the working end through the Figure 8 Knot.

Part Five

Loop Knots

Loop knots are easy enough to understand, but difficult to define precisely. Like hitches, they are tied to fit around objects (or people), but they are not intended to bind objects together (that's the job of binding knots). Loop knots may be tied at the end of a rope or anywhere along its length (on a bight). They may be of a fixed size or they may be adjustable. Unlike a hitch, which is tied on an object and depends upon that object for its structure, loop knots may be tied in the rope itself and then placed on the object when finished. Loop knots are useful for lifting and pulling objects and, in the form of a safety harness or bosun's chair, to lift or secure people as well. (Observe all safety recommendations in this book when using rope for these purposes.) A pair of interconnected loop knots can also be used in place of a bend to make a strong and durable connection between the ends of two ropes.

26. Double Overhand Loop

Uses: lifting, hauling, hanging gear from doubled line

Pros: easy to tie; works well with small stuff

Cons: difficult to untie; only appropriate on a bight

Page: 90

27. Figure 8 Loop

Uses: lifting, pulling, hanging loop for gear; tie-in point for climbers

Pros: easy to tie in rope of any thickness; fairly easy to untie; very strong

Cons: not as easy to untie as a Bowline

Page: 91

28. Threaded Figure 8 Loop

Uses: lifting, pulling, hanging loop for gear; belaying climbers

Pros: very strong and secure

Cons: fussy to tie

Page: 92

29. Directional Figure 8 Loop

Uses: climbing, lifting, load bearing

Pros: easily tied; very strong

Cons: will slip if loaded in wrong direction; dangerous to careless users; hard to untie

Page: 94

30. Fisherman's Loop

Uses: general-purpose tie-off or hanging point; fishing tackle

Pros: easy to tie; relatively secure

Cons: hard to make with a small loop; difficult to untie in small stuff; may slip

Page: 95

31. Double Overhand Sliding Loop

Uses: fishing, general-purpose noose

Pros: easy to tie; works well with small stuff; tightens easily

Cons: difficult to untie

Page: 96

32. Angler's Loop

Uses: fishing leaders, tippets and hooks, loops in bungee cord

Pros: holds well in any material

Cons: very difficult to untie; hard to fair and tighten in heavy rope

Page: 98

33. Bowline

Uses: lifting, connecting rope ends, sail-to-sheet connections, docklines

Pros: secure under load; easy to tie and untie

Cons: can capsize if not loaded; not the most secure form of bowline

Page: 100

34. Bowline with Stopper

Uses: lifting, personal safety, connecting rope ends; sail-to-sheet connections, docklines

Pros: more secure than standard Bowline; controls excessively long working end

Cons: more time-consuming than standard Bowline

Page: 101

35. Dutch Bowline

Uses: lifting large, heavy loads

Pros: working end is on outside of loop, unlike standard Bowline

Cons: less secure than standard Bowline

Page: 102

36. Bowline with Two Turns

Uses: general lifting, climbing, personal safety

Pros: very secure, easy to untie

Cons: bulkier than standard Bowline; requires more rope

Page: 104

37. Water Bowline

Uses: general lifting and pulling, safety; docklines, especially in wet, slippery rope

Pros: extremely secure

Cons: uses more rope, trickier to tie than regular Bowline

Page: 106

38. Portuguese Bowline

Uses: lifting large, heavy loads

Pros: secure, adjustable size loops, unties readily

Cons: loops can shift

Page: 107

39. Eskimo Bowline

Uses: lifting, pulling, safety; may be used as a hitch

Pros: very secure, especially in slippery rope

Cons: tricky to tie and fair

Page: 108

40. Bowline on a Bight

Uses: lifting, hauling, safety, climbing

Pros: very secure and strong, easy to untie, can use one or both loops

Cons: insecure if both standing parts are not loaded

Page: 110

41. Spanish Bowline

Uses: lifting large heavy loads, bosun's chair, or rescue harness

Pros: loops will not shift under load

Cons: difficult to tie with loops of unequal size

Page: 112

42. Alpine Butterfly

Uses: mid-rope tie-off point, purchase for tightening a line

Pros: easy and quick to tie; suitable for loads in either direction

Cons: only useful on a bight; awkward to tie large loops

Page: 114

26. Double Overhand Loop

Also known as: Overhand Loop, Loop Knot, Double Overhand Knot on a Bight

As easy to tie as a Double Overhand Knot (p.51), to which it is very closely related, the Double Overhand Loop shares the liability of most overhand knots in being difficult to untie. It is one of the easiest ways to form a loop on a bight, and fairly attractive withal.

Uses: lifting, hauling, and hanging gear from doubled line

Pros: easy to tie; works well in small stuff

Cons: difficult to untie; only appropriate on a bight

Instructions

1. Make an Overhand Knot (p.48) with a bight.

2. Bring the bight around the standing parts.

3. Pass the bight a second time through the crossing turn to complete the Double Overhand Knot on the bight.

4. Pull the loop against the two standing parts to tighten. Fair the knot by laying the four crossing turns close against each other.

Untying: Pry the doubled crossing turns apart, two of the strands toward the standing parts and the other two toward the end of the loop. Then draw the loop through the closer pair of crossing turns.

27. **Figure 8 Loop**

Also known as: Figure 8 on a Bight, Double (or Doubled) Figure 8 Knot, Flemish Loop

This fixed loop is tied just like a Figure 8 Knot (p.60), but on a bight. The bight may be placed near the working end of the rope or anywhere along its length. Tied in the middle, it provides a good tie-off point at the bottom of a rope that has been doubled for strength. The knot reduces the strength of the rope less than most other loop knots.

Uses: lifting, pulling, hanging gear; belaying climbers

Pros: very easy to tie in stuff of any thickness; fairly easy to untie; very strong

Cons: not as easy to untie as a Bowline

Instructions

1. Make a bight anywhere along the rope. Make a counterclockwise underhand crossing turn in the bight.

2. Take the end of the bight over the doubled rope.

3. Pass the bight through the doubled crossing turn from back to front to complete the figure 8.

4. Fair the knot so the doubled strands are parallel all the way through.

Untying: Pull the loop back through the first crossing turn toward the standing part.

28. **Threaded Figure 8 Loop**

This variation on the Figure 8 Loop (p.91) is tied with the working end, not on a bight, so it can be used to tie off to closed rings, or to make a loop around an object whose end is not accessible. It creates a fixed single loop.

Uses: lifting, pulling, hanging loop for gear; belaying climbers

Pros: very strong and secure

Cons: fussy to tie

Instructions

1. Start with a standard Figure 8 Knot (p.60), leaving a working end somewhat longer than the desired loop. Pass the working end through the ring or around the tie-off point to form the loop.

2. Thread the working end back through the upper crossing turn, next to and parallel with the working end where it exits the figure 8, but in the opposite direction.

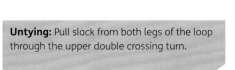

Untying: Pull slack from both legs of the loop through the upper double crossing turn.

3. Pass the working end behind the standing part, always working parallel to the course of the figure 8.

4. Pass the working end through the upper crossing turn of the figure 8, threading it beneath the two strands that form the loop.

5. Still working parallel to the original figure 8, pass the working end around both legs of the loop, then back down through the (now doubled) lower crossing turn, parallel with the standing part.

6. To tighten, hold the working end together with the standing part and pull against the loop. Then release the working end and pull the standing part against the loop.

29. Directional Figure 8 Loop

Also known as: Inline 8

Tied on a bight, the Directional Figure 8 Loop is meant to bear weight in one direction only. In this role it excels and is favored by climbers. Beware of applying weight in the other direction, however, for the knot will capsize and slide, functioning as an unintentional noose.

Uses: climbing, lifting, load bearing

Pros: easily tied; very strong

Cons: will slip if load is applied in the wrong direction; dangerous to careless users; difficult to untie if tightened hard

Instructions

Untying: Load must be removed from the knot before it can be untied. Pull the loop up through the crossing turn.

1. The working end is at the bottom of the photograph. Make a bight in the working end a little longer than the desired loop and pass it under the standing part, forming a counterclockwise crossing turn.

2. Bring the bight forward and across the standing part.

3. Pass the bight through the crossing turn from back to front.

4. Pull the bight through the crossing turn.

5. Pull both sides of the loop evenly against the standing part to tighten. If tied with a long working end, make sure that the loop bears weight only on the standing part.

30. Fisherman's Loop

Also known as: Middleman's Knot, Fisherman's Eye, Englishman's Loop

This is another fixed loop that can be tied either at the end or on a bight. Composed of two Overhand Knots (p.48), it is simple to tie but a little tricky to get the size of the loop exactly as desired.

Uses: general-purpose tie-off or hanging point; fishing tackle

Pros: easy to tie; relatively secure

Cons: hard to make with a small loop; difficult to untie in small stuff; may slip

Instructions

Untying: Slide the two Overhand Knots apart, untie the second one, and pull the drawloop through.

1. Make a counterclockwise overhand crossing turn. Form a bight near the working end and pass it through the turn from back to front. In other words, make a Slipped Overhand Knot (p.49) and draw it tight.

2. Make a clockwise underhand crossing turn with the working end around the standing part.

3. Pass the working end through the crossing turn to form an Overhand Knot (p.48).

4. Pull the working-end leg of the loop against the standing part of the line to draw the overhand knots against each other.

5. The finished knot.

31. **Double Overhand Sliding Loop**

This knot is popular among anglers to attach swivels and hooks. When tied in monofilament line, it draws up tight with little effort.

Uses: fishing, general-purpose noose

Pros: easy to tie; works well with small stuff; tightens easily

Cons: difficult to untie

Instructions

1. Make an overhand counterclockwise crossing turn.

2. Bring the working end around the back to form a crossing turn around the standing part.

Untying: Don't plan on untying this knot. It's best used for monofilament or other small stuff that you plan to cut.

3. Bring the working end forward to form a round turn around the base of the loop.

31. **Double Overhand Sliding Loop**

4. Pass the working end behind the loop and bring it forward again.

5. Pass the working end through the round turn and the crossing turn.

6. Pull the working end against the working-end leg of the loop to secure the knot, as shown. Then pull the standing part of the rope against the working-end leg of the loop to tighten the noose.

32. Angler's Loop

Also known as: Perfection Loop

Tied in any kind of small stuff, this fixed loop will not slip. It works well with monofilament, bungee cord, and regular cordage. It is difficult to tie in heavier rope but it holds well in that too—so well, in fact, that you should consider it fairly permanent, no matter the type or size of cordage. Usually tied on the working end, it can also be tied on the bight.

Uses: fishing leaders, tippets and hooks, bungee cord, bungeed tent fly tie-downs

Pros: holds well in any material

Cons: very difficult to untie; hard to fair and tighten in heavy rope

Instructions

1. Make a bight of the desired size. (The bight is not the loop, but the loop will be the same size.) Bring the working end forward to create a crossing turn around the standing part.

2. Bring the working end behind the bight.

3. Bring the working end across the front of the bight one more time, completing a round turn.

Untying: Got a knife?

98

4. Holding the working end down, reach through the bight from back to front with the other hand, grab the crossing turn, and pull it across the working end.

5. Continue pulling the crossing turn through the bight from front to back, pulling all of the slack out of the bight and forming the loop.

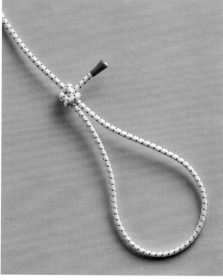

6. Tighten the knot by holding the standing part in one hand, using the other hand to pull the crossing turn through the bight until the bight locks down on the loop.

7. When tying the Angler's Loop in bungee cord, the knot must be faired carefully as it is tightened or it may collapse under load.

33. **Bowline**

Also known as: Bowline Loop, Bowline Knot

The bowline is one of the most useful fixed-size loops. It is strong, easy to tie in the end of a rope, and it can be readily untied no matter how tight it has been pulled. It has many variations, several of which follow.

Uses: general lifting, connecting ends of two ropes, sail-to-sheet connections, docklines

Pros: secure under load; easy to tie, easy to untie

Cons: can capsize if not under load; may slip; not the most secure form of bowline

Instructions

Untying: Pull up on the bight that goes around the standing part to free the working end from the crossing turn.

1. Make a counterclockwise overhand crossing turn, leaving a working end long enough to form the loop and complete the knot.

2. Pass the working end through the crossing turn from back to front.

3. Pass the working end behind the standing end.

4. Bring the working end down through the crossing turn from front to back.

5. To tighten, pull the standing part against the leg of the loop closer to the working end.

34. Bowline with Stopper

Also known as: Bowline Loop or Bowline Knot with End Secured

As good a knot as the Bowline is, it can slip if tied in slippery rope. An Overhand Knot (p.48) tied in the working end around one strand of the loop will help prevent this. It is also a good way to make the knot tidier if the working end is too long.

Uses: general lifting, personal safety, connecting ends of two ropes, sail-to-sheet connections, docklines

Pros: increases security of Bowline; controls excessively long working end

Cons: bulkier and more time-consuming than standard Bowline

Instructions

Untying: Untie the Overhand Knot, then pull the bight up along the standing part to free the working end from the crossing turn.

1. Tie a standard Bowline (opposite), leaving a longer working end than usual. Make an underhand crossing turn around the working-end leg of the loop.

2. Bring the working end forward, and pass it through the crossing turn from front to back to form an Overhand Knot. Hold the standing part of the rope above the Bowline, and pull the Overhand Knot down and tighten.

35. One-handed Bowline

Also known as: Bowline Loop, Bowline Knot

Climbers occasionally need to tie a Bowline (p.100) with one hand because the other is occupied holding on to something for dear life. This method requires good manual dexterity, but it produces a standard Bowline with all its virtues.

Uses: general lifting, personal safety, connecting ends of two ropes, sail-to-sheet connections, docklines

Pros: secure; easy to tie, easy to untie

Cons: can capsize and slip; not the most secure form of bowline

Instructions

1. Form the body of the loop in the working end of the rope, then make a bight at the very end. (The bight is optional; it doesn't form a part of the knot, but it's easier to manipulate the working end this way.)

2. Holding the bight with your palm down, use your thumb to lift the standing part of the loop.

Untying: Pull up on the bight that goes around the standing part to free the working end from the crossing turn.

3. Twist your wrist up so that the standing part of the loop forms a counterclockwise overhand crossing turn over the bight in the working end. Be careful that the crossing turn does not form over your wrist, or you could find yourself entrapped.

35. One-handed Bowline

4. Undo the bight and pass the working end behind the standing part.

5. Pull the working end through the crossing turn from front to back.

6. Continue to pull the working end through the crossing turn. Depending upon how large you want the loop, you might hold both strands of the new bight that you've created around the rope's standing part and pull them together through the crossing turn.

7. The finished Bowline.

36. **Dutch Bowline**

Also known as: Backward Bowline

This slight variation of the standard Bowline (p.100) positions the working end outside the loop. It is said to be somewhat less secure than a standard Bowline, but it does place the loop in more complete contact with the object it surrounds. If used as a safety line, it's more comfortable this way, with the working end away from the torso.

Uses: lifting large, heavy loads
Pros: secure; unties readily
Cons: less secure than standard Bowline

Instructions

1. Begin like a standard Bowline. Leaving a long working end, make a small overhand counterclockwise crossing turn and pass the working end through the crossing turn from back to front. As the working end passes through the crossing turn, pass it perpendicular to the standing part.

2. Pass the working end behind the standing part and bring it forward.

Untying: Untie like a standard Bowline: lift the bight along the working part until the working end is free of the crossing turn.

3. Bring the working end back through the crossing turn from front to back.

4. Tighten by pulling on the standing part and working end.

5. The finished knot, with the working end on the outside of the loop.

37. Bowline with Two Turns

Also known as: Double Bowline, Round Turn Bowline

Another bowline variation, this one is stronger, more resistant to slippage, and resists capsizing better. Climbers rely on it for safety. After you've learned the standard Bowline (p.100), this one's simple: just replace the initial crossing turn with two round turns.

Uses: general lifting, climbing, personal safety

Pros: very secure; easy to untie

Cons: bulkier than standard Bowline; requires more rope

Instructions

1. Make two counterclockwise round turns in the standing part, leaving the working end long enough to form the loop and complete the knot.

2. Pass the working end through the round turns from back to front.

Untying: Grab the upper round turn and pull some slack from the standing-part leg of the loop. Then pull the bight up along the rope's standing part to release the working end.

3. Pass the working end behind the standing part and bring it forward.

4. Pass the working end through the round turns from front to back.

5. Pull the working end and the standing part to tighten. The knot may need to be faired by pulling the standing-part leg of the loop against the standing part of the rope.

38. Water Bowline

Probably the most secure bowline, the Water Bowline forms two Half Hitches (p.56) around the bight in the working end. It's especially useful to maintain security in wet, slippery line, yet it can still be untied easily.

Uses: general lifting and pulling, safety, docklines, especially in wet, slippery rope

Pros: extremely secure

Cons: uses more rope; trickier to tie than regular Bowline

Instructions

1. Make two counterclockwise overhand crossing turns in the standing part, leaving the working end long enough to form the loop and complete the knot.

2. Shift the lower crossing turn (the one closer to the working end) under the upper one and hold them together.

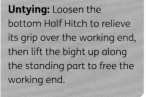

Untying: Loosen the bottom Half Hitch to relieve its grip over the working end, then lift the bight up along the standing part to free the working end.

3. The rest of the procedure is the same as a standard Bowline (p.100). Pass the working end through the crossing turns from back to front, then behind the standing part.

4. Pass the working end through the crossing turns from front to back. Hold both ends of the bight together in one hand while pulling on the standing part of the rope to tighten the upper Half Hitch. Then pull the standing-part leg of the loop to tighten the lower Half Hitch.

5. The finished Water Bowline. If the working end is too long, it may be secured with an Overhand Knot around the loop, as in the Bowline with Stopper Knot (p.63).

39. Portuguese Bowline

Also known as: French Bowline

This double-loop bowline is tied at the working end, not on a bight. It can be tied with both loops of equal size or in any proportion desired for balanced lifting of odd-sized loads. It can be used as a bosun's chair with two equal loops around the legs. The bosun's chair is sometimes arranged with one loop around both legs and the other around the torso, but this is dangerous and so not advisable.

Uses: lifting large, heavy loads

Pros: secure; adjustable size loops; unties readily

Cons: loops can shift toward the one bearing the heavier load

Instructions

Untying: Untie like a standard Bowline: lift the bight along the working part until the working end is free of the crossing turn.

1. The knot begins just like a standard Bowline (p.100), but with the working end long enough to form two loops. Make a counterclockwise crossing turn. Pass the long working end through the crossing turn from back to front and pull it through to form the first loop.

2. Pass the working end through the crossing turn a second time, again from back to front.

3. Pass the working end behind the standing part and bring it forward.

4. The working end now goes back down through the crossing turn from front to back.

5. Adjust the size of the two loops as needed, then pull the standing part against the working end to tighten and knot and lock the loops.

40. Eskimo Bowline

Also known as: Boas Bowline

Although similar in its final form to a standard Bowline (p.100), this knot is tied quite differently, so it's best to approach it as something new. It is trickier to tie and fair than a standard Bowline, but it is said to be more secure. It is reliably reported as being of true Inuit (i.e., Eskimo) origin, and was tied in rawhide as hitches to assemble dogsleds.

Uses: lifting, pulling, safety; may be used as a hitch

Pros: very secure, especially in synthetic line

Cons: tricky to tie and fair

Instructions

1. Leaving a long working end, make a counterclockwise overhand crossing turn in the standing part.

2. Pass the working end through the crossing turn from front to back.

3. Take the working end behind the standing part then bring it forward.

40. Eskimo Bowline

4. Pass the working end through the crossing turn again, this time from back to front.

5. Tighten by pulling simultaneously on both parts of the bight in the working end and the standing part of the rope.

6. The finished knot. When properly faired, the working end forms a neat bight with adjacent, parallel legs.

Untying: After tension is released on the knot, the working end may be readily pulled through the crossing turn.

41. Bowline on a Bight

The diverse and immensely useful bowline family deserves an "on the bight" version. This knot has the advantages of a standard Bowline (p.100) with the additional benefit of doubled line in both the standing part and in the loop for extra strength and reliability. It can't possibly slip, and the two fixed-size loops can fit around your thighs as part of a harness for climbing, rescue, or raising a sailor up a mast.

Uses: lifting, hauling, safety, climbing

Pros: very secure and strong, easy to untie; loops may be used together or separately

Cons: relies on both strands of the standing part for support; don't haul or support with only one strand

Instructions

1. Make a counterclockwise overhand crossing turn in a bight and then bring the bight through the crossing turn from back to front to form a loose Overhand Loop (p.53). Unlike a standard Bowline, it is the initial crossing turn that will become the final load-bearing loops, so size it accordingly. (We'll call the initial crossing turn the "loops" henceforth, because another crossing turn will be formed presently.)

2. Bring the bight down toward the bottom of the loops.

41. Bowline on a Bight

3. Open up the bight wide and pass it under the loops.

4. Bring the opened bight up behind the loops.

5. Bring the bight completely over the top of the loops and around the standing parts.

6. Holding both loops high near the rope's standing parts in one hand, tighten the knot by pulling the other end of both loops (near the bight). This will form a new crossing turn in the bight around the standing parts.

7. The finished knot.

Untying: Untying this knot is simply the reverse of tying it. Raise the bight along the standing parts and pull it until it's large enough to pass toward the back and bring it forward over the two loops.

42. Spanish Bowline

Also known as: French Bowline, Double Forked Loop, Chair Knot

This is another double-looped bowline on a bight, offering nearly double the strength of a single Bowline (p.100) plus the ability to spread a load evenly across two loops. The loops will not shift or tighten under load, and with one's legs placed through the loops, it makes a good bosun's chair or rescue harness, although you have to hold onto the standing parts (or tie your upper body to them with another piece of line) to keep from falling out backward.

Uses: lifting large heavy loads, bosun's chair, or rescue harness

Pros: loops will not shift under load

Cons: difficult to tie with loops of unequal size

Instructions

1. Middle the rope, then pull the bight beneath the two standing parts, creating two opposing crossing turns.

2. Twist both crossing turns inward 180 degrees around their standing parts, to form elbows in both legs.

Untying: Pull both standing parts through the bight that surrounds them on their way into the knot. Once this is loose, pull either loop out from beneath the standing parts, then pull the other loop through the first one.

42. Spanish **Bowline**

3. Overlap the two crossing turns with the right one over the left. Grab the right leg of the left crossing turn through the right crossing turn and pull it through.

4. With the original left crossing turn pulled through the original right one, there is now a new crossing turn around the standing parts.

5. Reach through the backs of the original twin crossing turns. Grab the right leg of the third crossing turn with the right hand; grab the left side of the third crossing turn with the left hand.

6. Pull both sides of the third crossing turn through the original twin crossing turns to form two loops.

7. Pull the loops tight to finish the knot.

43. **Alpine Butterfly**

Also known as: Alpine Butterfly Loop, Lineman's Loop

This is a quick, easy loop to tie on a bight. It's used by mountaineers to create a tie-in point for a third climber between two others climbers. It serves well as a purchase for lashing boats or cargo to a car's roof rack and for making a line tight between two trees, to serve as a clothesline or a tarp ridgeline.

Uses: mid-rope tie-off point, purchase for tightening a line

Pros: easy and quick to tie, suitable for loads in either direction

Cons: only useful on a bight, awkward to tie for large loops

Instructions

1. Make two round turns around one hand. With the two ends facing opposite directions, there will be three "strands" in total over your hand.

2. Take the left strand and pass it over the middle one, so that it becomes the new middle strand.

Untying: The loop is held by two opposing crossing turns. Lever the one that's farther from the standing parts down toward the loop, then pull the loop through. Then pull the loop through the second crossing turn.

3. Pull slack into the new left strand (originally the middle one) large enough for the loop.

43. Alpine Butterfly

4. Pass this new left strand over the other two strands. We'll call this strand the loop henceforth.

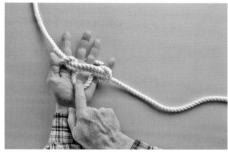

5. Pull the loop beneath and through the other two strands.

6. Hold both standing parts in one hand and pull the loop tight.

7. The finished knot will bear a load from either standing part and from the loop itself.

Part Six
Bends

Bends are used to tie the ends of two—or occasionally three—ropes together. In accomplishing this, a bend is generally an easier, quicker, and less bulky solution than tying two loop knots through one another. Some bends work best with ropes of similar diameter, while others are optimized for ropes of different sizes, and some work well in flat materials such as leather straps or nylon webbing.

44. Water Knot

Uses: load bearing; bending flat materials or rope

Pros: easy to tie; secure; straps remain flat

Cons: difficult to untie in rope

Page: 119

45. Sheet Bend

Uses: temporary light-duty applications where constant load will be maintained

Pros: simple to tie and untie in ropes of equal or different diameter

Cons: insecure when unloaded

Page: 120

46. Double Sheet Bend

Uses: joining lines of dissimilar diameters; connecting heaving and messenger lines

Pros: less prone to slippage than a Sheet Bend; easy to tie and untie

Cons: relatively insecure when unloaded; may catch on obstructions if it will be dragged

Page: 121

47. Tucked Sheet Bend

Uses: joining two lines that will be dragged or towed; dinghy painters; towlines

Pros: reduced chance of catching on obstruction, less drag when towed in water

Cons: somewhat insecure if not kept under load

Page: 122

48. Three-way Sheet Bend

Uses: two-to-one or one-to-two towing

Pros: an easy three-way bend; easy to untie; works with different size ropes

Cons: insecure

Page: 123

49. Flemish Bend

Uses: standing rigging, static and dynamic loads

Pros: secure

Cons: difficult to untie in natural fiber rope; only for ropes of equal diameter

Page: 124

50. Double Figure 8 Bend

Uses: joining ropes for climbing, mountaineering

Pros: very secure and strong, absorbs shock

Cons: none known

Page: 126

51. Carrick Bend

Uses: joining heavy, stiff ropes

Pros: more secure than Sheet Bend or Reef Knot, easy to untie

Cons: reduces rope strength considerably

Page: 127

52. Zeppelin Bend

Uses: load lifting, safety

Pros: strong; remains secure when unloaded; easily untied

Cons: tricky to tie; bulky; may catch when dragged

Page: 128

53. Hunter's Bend

Uses: load bearing

Pros: remains secure with or without load; holds slippery rope well

Cons: fussy to tie in hand; hard to untie

Page: 130

54. Ashley's Bend

Uses: load bearing in thin rope, bungee cord

Pros: very secure

Cons: fussy to tie in hand, difficult to check; hard to untie

Page: 132

55. Fisherman's Knot

Uses: joining small or medium cordage

Pros: easy and quick to tie

Cons: can capsize or slip under tension; difficult to untie

Page: 133

56. Double Fisherman's Knot

Uses: joining cordage of any weight, including monofilament and anchor lines

Pros: easy to tie, quite secure

Cons: difficult to untie

Page: 134

57. Blood Knot

Uses: joining ends of rope of any weight, especially monofilament

Pros: very secure, simple in concept

Cons: difficult to manipulate, very difficult to untie

Page: 136

44. Water Knot

Also known as: Double Overhand Bend, Tape Knot, Tape Bend

This knot works well with flat stuff like nylon webbing and leather straps as well as with conventional rope. It's used by climbers, but also practical for extending the length of cargo tie-down straps.

Uses: load bearing; joining ends of straps, webbing, and ropes

Pros: easy to tie, secure; straps remain flat

Cons: difficult to untie in rope

Instructions

Untying: Pry the two crossing turns away from each other, then pull the working ends through the crossing turns.

1. Tie an Overhand Knot (p.48) near the working end of one strap or rope. Working from the opposite direction, thread the other line's working end through the Overhand Knot, parallel to the first working end.

2. Continue threading the second working end parallel to and around the first Overhand Knot so that it forms its own Overhand Knot.

3. Pull the working ends to remove slack, then pull the standing parts to tighten.

4. When tying in straps or webbing, keep the two lines flat, untwisted, and parallel to one another all the way through the knot.

5. To keep flat materials from bunching up, the knot must be tightened gradually and continually faired.

45. **Sheet Bend**

Also known as: Basket Hitch, Weaver's Knot

The Sheet Bend is simple to tie but rather insecure, especially if a constant load is not maintained. It forms the basis for several knots that are more secure, so it's an important one to learn. Often used to join lines of different diameters, it actually holds better in lines of equal size.

Uses: temporary pulling or static applications where load will be maintained

Pros: simple to tie and untie in ropes of equal or different diameter

Cons: insecure

Instructions

Untying: Pull the working end out from the crossing turn.

1. Make a bight in one rope. If the two ropes are of different diameters, make the bight in the heavier one. Pass the working end of the other rope through the bight from back to front, then around the bight, going first over the working end before coming back to the front over the standing part.

2. Pass the working end of the second rope under itself. The second rope will form an underhand crossing turn over the bight of the first rope. Make sure both working ends exit the knot on the same side.

3. Pull the two standing parts to tighten.

46. Double Sheet Bend

Also known as: Doubled Basket Hitch or Weaver's Knot

Less prone to slippage and more secure than the standard Sheet Bend (opposite), the doubled version is especially useful where one rope is significantly heavier than the other or so stiff that it cannot be bent into a small radius for other types of bends.

Uses: joining lines of dissimilar diameters; connecting a heaving or messenger line to a dock line or safety rope

Pros: less prone to slippage than a Sheet Bend, easy to tie and untie

Cons: May be insecure if not kept under load; may catch on obstructions if it will be dragged

Instructions

Untying: Pull the working end of the thinner line from the second crossing turn, then pull it from the first.

1. Tie a standard Sheet Bend, using a longer working end with the thinner rope. Pass the working end around the bight in the bigger rope, going first around the working end of the bight, then around its standing part before bringing it forward again.

2. Pass the working end of the thinner rope beneath its own standing part, so that there are two crossing turns around the bight.

3. Pull the two standing parts to tighten.

47. Tucked Sheet Bend

Also known as: One-way Sheet Bend

This version of the Sheet Bend (p.120) uses a Figure 8 Knot (p.60) to reverse the direction of the working end of the thinner rope, so that it faces the same way as the working end of the larger rope. With both working ends facing away from the direction of movement, the knot is less likely to catch on an obstruction if the line is dragged along the ground, and it will create less drag if towed through the water behind a boat.

Uses: joining two lines that will be dragged or towed; dinghy painters or other towlines

Pros: more secure than standard Sheet Bend; reduced chance of catching on obstruction; less drag when towed in water

Cons: insecure if not under load

Instructions

1. Tie a standard Sheet Bend.

2. Bring the working end of the thinner rope back around its own standing part.

Untying: Pull the working end of the thinner line out of the two crossing turns in sequence to undo the Figure 8 Knot.

3. Tuck the working end through the crossing turn at the end of the thinner rope from back to front. This completes a Figure 8 Knot in the thinner rope.

4. Hold both parts of the bight in the thicker rope together with the working end of the thinner rope. Pull the standing part of the thinner rope to tighten.

5. The finished knot.

48. Three-way Sheet Bend

This knot can be used to form a towrope joined to a bridle between the port and starboard stern cleats on a boat. Used in the opposite way (with the single line as the anchor and the other two lines trailing), a single strong paddler could tow two weaker ones. It is insecure and prone to slippage, but this can be remedied by finishing the knot as a Tucked Sheet Bend (opposite).

Uses: two-to-one or one-to-two towing

Pros: one of few easy three-way bends; easy to tie and untie; works with different diameter ropes

Cons: insecure and subject to slipping

Instructions

Untying: Pull the working ends of the thinner ropes out from under the parallel crossing turns.

1. Make a bight with the thicker rope. Keeping the two thinner ropes parallel, pass their working ends through the bight from back to front, around the bight's working end, and then around the standing part of the bight, bringing the two working ends forward.

2. Tuck both thinner working ends beneath their own standing parts.

3. To tighten, pull both parts of the bight with one hand, and the standing parts of both thinner ropes with the other. If a tucked finish is desired, the two thinner ropes may be brought forward and passed through their own crossing turn from back to front, so that all three working ends face the same direction.

49. Flemish Bend

Also known as: Flemish Knot, Figure 8 Bend

Popular among climbers and sailors, the Flemish Bend is two intertwined or "threaded" Figure 8 Knots (also known as Flemish Knots, p.60) tied in ropes of equal diameter. It's difficult to untie in natural fiber, but easy enough in slipperier synthetic.

Uses: static rigging

Pros: more secure than most sheet bends

Cons: difficult to untie in natural fiber rope; only for ropes of equal diameters

Instructions

1. Tie a Figure 8 Knot in the end of one of the ropes.

2. Pull a long working end of the other rope through the first crossing turn of the first Figure 8, parallel to the first one's working end but from the opposite direction.

Untying: Grab one pair of crossing turns in each hand and flex the knot back and forth until they loosen. Then pull both working ends through the crossing turns.

3. Use the second working end to follow the first figure 8 around in parallel. Go over the first rope's standing part and follow its second crossing turn, going next through its first crossing turn from back to front.

49. Flemish Bend

4. Keep following the first figure 8 with the second working end. The last move takes it back through the second crossing turn of the first rope from front to back.

5. The threaded nature of the knot is apparent before tightening. Both lines run parallel throughout.

6. Tightening requires holding one standing part and pulling alternately on the two strands on the opposite end of the knot, then switching to hold the other standing part and pulling alternately "new" opposite ends.

50. Double Figure 8 Bend

Also known as: Flemish Bend

One of the most secure bends, this is a favorite climbing knot because of its great strength and ability to absorb shock loads. Like the Flemish Bend (p.124), it's composed of two Figure 8 Knots (p.60), but here each one is tied around the standing part of the other rope, rather than being threaded together.

Uses: joining ropes for climbing, mountaineering

Pros: very secure and strong, absorbs shock loads

Cons: none known

Instructions

1. Tie a Figure 8 Knot in one rope. Turn it over if necessary, so the working end emerges from the first crossing turn from back to front. Pass the working end of the other rope through the figure 8's first crossing turn from front to back, parallel with the first working end but in the opposite direction.

2. Make an underhand clockwise crossing turn with the second rope's working end around the first rope's standing part.

Untying: Pull the two figure 8s away from each other, then untie each separately.

3. Finish the second figure 8 by taking the working end over the front of its own standing part, then drawing it through its first crossing turn from back to front. Tighten both figure 8s separately.

4. Pull the two standing parts to draw the figure 8s together. The two may also be left some inches apart as shown, to absorb shock loads.

5. The finished knot with the two figure 8s drawn together.

51. **Carrick Bend**

Also known as: Carrick Bend with Ends Adjacent, Double Carrick Bend, Josephine Knot

Composed entirely of large-radius curves, the Carrick Bend is ideal for joining the ends of stiff ropes of equal diameters that can't take tight curves. This version places the working ends next to each other when it is tightened. Another version, the Carrick Bend with Ends Opposed, has the working ends pointing in opposite directions and is strictly for decorative use—hence not included here.

Uses: joining heavy, stiff ropes

Pros: stronger and more secure than a Sheet Bend or Square Knot; won't jam

Cons: none known

Instructions (NB R1 = Rope 1, R2 = Rope 2)

Untying: Each working end is captured by a bight in the standing part of the same rope. Starting with either rope, push the bight in the direction of the standing part, then pull slack from the standing part, and finally remove the working end of the opposite rope.

1. Lay the two ropes with working ends facing. Make an underhand clockwise crossing turn in the rope on the right (R1). Pass the standing part of R2 beneath the crossing turn, and take its working end over the standing part and under the working end of R1.

2. Bring the working end of R2 over the standing-part leg of the crossing turn in R1 and under its own standing part.

3. Pull the working end of R2 over the opposite leg of the crossing turn in R1 to complete the second of the interlocking crossing turns.

4. Pull both standing parts to tighten.

5. The knot will capsize as it tightens, losing some of the visual appeal it has when loose, but becoming very secure.

52. **Zeppelin Bend**

Also known as: Rosendahl's Knot

This is a very strong, secure knot that will snug up and fair itself nicely when first placed under load. It works well in equal-size cordage of any diameter and can be easily untied, but the working ends sticking out in opposite directions at right angles to the standing parts make it inappropriate for dragging over ground or towing through water.

Uses: load lifting, safety

Pros: strong; remains secure when unloaded; easily untied

Cons: tricky to tie; bulky; may catch when dragged

Instructions (NB R1 = Rope 1, R2 = Rope 2)

1. Place the two ropes next to each other, facing the same direction. Make an overhand clockwise crossing turn in the lower one (hereafter, R1) so that its working end passes over R2.

2. Bring the working end of R1 behind both standing parts and tie a loose Overhand Knot (p.48) around R2.

3. Holding the two ropes together at the Overhand Knot, pull a bight into the standing part of R2 below the knot.

52. **Zeppelin Bend**

4. Pull the working end of R2 through the bight from back to front.

5. Pull the working end of R2 through the Overhand Knot from front to back.

6. Hold both standing parts together in one hand and pull the two working ends tight with the other.

7. The knot assumes its proper shape after the two standing parts are pulled tight in opposite directions.

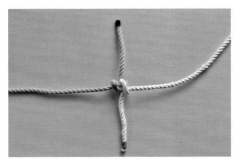

Untying: The knot ends with what are essentially two Half Hitches (p.56) locking the two working ends against each other. Alternately, they may be viewed as turns around their own standing parts and the first crossing turn of the other rope. Whatever you wish to call them, pull them in opposite directions to loosen the knot.

8. The opposite side of the finished knot.

53. **Hunter's Bend**

Also known as: Rigger's Bend

With its working ends facing in opposite directions, perpendicular to the standing parts, the Hunter's Bend resembles the Zeppelin Bend (p.128). Because the opposing crossing turns must remain parallel before tightening, it is best tied on a flat surface. For years it was used by riggers and climbers and not by hunters, but it was popularized by a Dr. Hunter in the 1970s.

Uses: load bearing

Pros: remains secure with or without load; holds slippery rope well

Cons: fussy to tie in hand; jams

Instructions (NB R1 = Rope 1, R2 = Rope 2)

1. Lay out the two ropes with their working ends facing each other and overlapping by a foot (30 cm) or more, with the rope on the right (R1) above the one on the left (R2).

2. Make an overhand clockwise crossing turn with R1, then a counterclockwise underhand crossing turn with R2 parallel to and around the first one. The working ends will continue to face the same direction as in the original layout.

Untying: Each rope's working end is captured by a bight in its own standing part. Working with either rope, push the bight toward the standing part; pull slack from the standing part then free the working end of the other rope.

3. Pass the working end of R1 through both crossing turns from back to front.

4. Pass the working end of R2 through both crossing turns from front to back.

5. The knot before it is tightened.

6. Hold the working ends stationary between thumb and index finger as shown. Grab the standing parts between your other fingers and the heel of your hand, and pull the standing parts to remove all the slack.

7. The knot will collapse into its proper shape as the slack is removed. Pull the standing parts to tighten.

54. Ashley's Bend

Ashley's Bend is secure even if subjected to movement and unloading, and is one of the best for tying in thin stuff and bungee cord. Like the Hunter's Bend (p.130), it consists of two intertwined crossing turns, but in Ashley's case, the setup places the two ropes in the same direction. The finished knot is somewhat untidy but effective.

Uses: thin rope, bungee cord, general load bearing

Pros: very secure; unties easily

Cons: fussy to tie in hand; difficult to see if it's tied correctly; jams

Instructions (NB R1 = Rope 1, R2 = Rope 2)

1. Lay the two ropes side by side facing the same direction. Make a clockwise underhand crossing turn with the left rope (R1) around R2.

2. Make a clockwise underhand crossing turn with R2, placing the working end on top of the standing part of R1.

3. Take both working ends and pass them through both crossing turns from front to back.

Untying: Both working ends are held under a crossing turn of R2. Lever this down toward the working ends, then pull the ends free. R2 remains held by an Overhand Knot (p.48) in R1 which must then be loosened.

4. Pull both working ends against both standing parts to remove slack.

5. Pull the two standing parts to tighten. Fair the knot so that the working ends are parallel and adjacent, with each working end perpendicular and adjacent to its own standing part.

55. Fisherman's Knot

Also known as: True Lover's Knot, Water Knot, Waterman's Knot, English Knot, Englishman's Knot

This simple but effective bend consists of two Overhand Knots (p.48), each tied around the standing part of the other rope. The working ends may be taped against the standing parts for added security.

Uses: joining ends of small or medium cordage

Pros: easy and quick to tie

Cons: can capsize or slip under tension; difficult to untie

Instructions

Untying: Slide the two Overhand Knots apart and untie each separately.

1. With the ropes facing opposite directions, overlap their working ends by several inches. Tie an Overhand Knot in the working end of one rope around the standing part of the other.

2. Tie a second Overhand Knot in the second rope around the standing part of the first. Tighten both Overhand Knots.

3. Pull the standing parts to draw the Overhand Knots together.

4. The finished knot drawn tight.

56. **Double Fisherman's Knot**

Also known as: Grinner Knot, Grapevine Knot, Double English Knot

This simple variation on the Fisherman's Knot (p.133) places Double Overhand Knots (p.51) around the standing parts of the opposite rope. It is much more secure than the standard Fisherman's Knot and works better in larger rope.

Uses: joining ends of rope of any weight, including fishing monofilament and anchor lines

Pros: easy to tie; quite secure

Cons: difficult to untie

Instructions

1. With the ropes facing opposite directions, overlap their working ends by several inches. Make a crossing turn with one working end around the standing part of the other rope.

2. Make a round turn around the standing part, working back toward the first rope's standing part.

Untying: Slide the two Double Overhand Knots apart and untie each separately.

3. Pass the working end through the round turn and the crossing turn to finish the first Double Overhand Knot. Pull it tight.

56. Double Fisherman's Knot

4. Tie an identical Double Overhand Knot in the other working end around the first rope's standing part.

5. Pull the two standing parts to draw the Double Overhand Knots together.

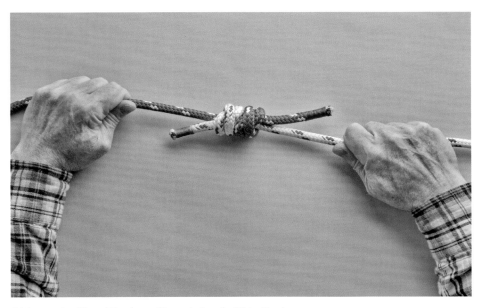

6. The completed knot. Trim the working ends short for fishing line; leave them long for load-bearing applications such as anchor lines.

57. **Blood Knot**

Also known as: Barrel Knot, Blood Knot with Inward Coil

This is a very popular fishing knot, but it works well in heavier stuff too. It snugs up so tight that it's quite difficult, if not impossible, to untie.

Uses: joining ends of rope of any weight, especially monofilament

Pros: very secure; simple in concept

Cons: difficult to manipulate; very difficult to untie under load

Instructions

1. With the ropes facing opposite directions, overlap their working ends. Make a crossing turn in one working end around the standing part of the other rope.

2. Pull the crossing turn tight and make a round turn around the other rope's standing part, working toward the first rope's standing part.

Untying: Consider this knot permanent. If you must attempt to untie it, try to pull the coils away from each other. That will free the working ends.

3. Keep wrapping round turns around the standing part of the second rope.

57. **Blood Knot**

4. With a minimum of five turns altogether (including the original crossing turn), pass the working end between its own standing part and the working end of the other rope.

5. Holding the first working end in place, make an identical set of crossing and round turns with the second working end around the standing part of the first rope. This requires some dexterity or a superabundance of fingers.

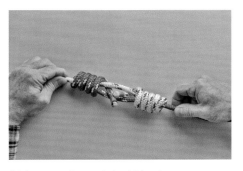

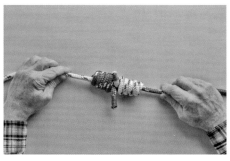

6. The two working ends should face the same direction between the standing parts as you pull on the standing parts to draw the coils together. If tying in monofilament, a drop of water or spit on the coils will help them slide more easily and tighten more securely.

7. The finished knot.

Part Seven
Hitches

Tie a hitch when you need to connect two objects with a length of rope. Unlike loop knots, in which the rope is tied to itself and is independent of the object encircled, hitches generally depend upon the object to which they are tied for their form and integrity: remove the object, and there is no knot. They are often tied around roughly cylindrical objects like trees, posts, rails, stakes, poles, bitts, and bollards.

58. Marlinespike Hitch

Uses: temporary "handle" for pulling line

Pros: quick, easy, unties instantly

Cons: strictly temporary; can slip

Page: 141

59. Round Turn and Two Half Hitches

Uses: hitch or adjustable noose for perpendicular loads, e.g., boats, tarp ridgelines

Pros: strong and fairly secure, easy to tie and untie, adjustable

Cons: can slip, adjustment not as secure as Taut Line Hitch

Page: 142

60. Turn and Two Half Hitches

Uses: hitch or adjustable noose for perpendicular loads, e.g., boats, clotheslines

Pros: uses less rope and easier to adjust than Round Turn version

Cons: somewhat less secure than Round Turn version

Page: 143

61. Taut Line Hitch

Uses: adjustable hitch; tent and fly guys, cargo tie-down, clotheslines, tarp ridgelines

Pros: tightens easily; holds adjustment better than Two Half Hitches

Cons: can slip, more complicated than Two Half Hitches

Page: 144

62. Buntline Hitch

Uses: halyards, sail sheets, tarp guy attachment, friction noose

Pros: very secure even if shaken

Cons: difficult to untie

Page: 146

63. Anchor Bend—Version 1

Uses: anchors, grapnels, hitching to a ring

Pros: very secure in slippery line; can be tied loose around the object

Cons: none known

Page: 147

64. Anchor Bend—Version 2

Uses: anchors, grapnels, hitching to a ring

Pros: strong, secure, more compact than Version 1

Cons: strain on rope is greater than Version 1

Page: 148

65., 66. Clove Hitch

Uses: light-duty hitch for boats, hanging gear; binding knot

Pros: easy and quick to tie

Cons: insecure; can jam

Pages: 149, 150 (on a bight)

67. Constrictor Knot

Uses: heavy-duty hitch in thin line; binding; seizing

Pros: very secure, easy to tie; ends can be cut short

Cons: very difficult to untie if tightened hard

Page: 151

68. Rolling Hitch

Uses: pulling or taking strain off another rope, securing a load in line with fixed object

Pros: secure and easy

Cons: insecure if load is perpendicular to object

Page: 152

69. Timber Hitch

Uses: hauling and lifting large heavy cylinders

Pros: simple to tie, easy to untie

Cons: insecure if load is perpendicular to object

Page: 153

70., 71., 72., 73. Cow Hitch

Uses: hitching animals; adding hanging loops or tie-offs to rails, rings, other ropes

Pros: easy and quick to tie by many methods, easy to untie; does not jam

Cons: insecure; unequal loads will shift

Pages: 154 (on a bight), 154 (in a loop), 155 (over the end), 155 (with one working end)

74. Pedigree Cow Hitch

Uses: hitching to rails, posts, and rings, hanging gear

Pros: only cow hitch with a single load-bearing part; secure in any direction

Cons: not among the most secure hitches; can be difficult to untie

Page: 156

75. Cow Hitch with Toggle

Uses: hanging gear from horizontal ropes or rails

Pros: quick and easy to tie and untie; works when only a bight is available

Cons: insecure; will slip if loaded unevenly; requires a toggle

Page: 157

76. Mooring Hitch

Uses: quick-release adjustable hitch for constant light loads

Pros: releases instantly and adjustable far from the fixed object

Cons: insecure

Page: 158

77. Highwayman's Hitch

Uses: quick-release hitch for boats or horses

Pros: releases instantly far from the fixed object

Cons: insecure; not adjustable like the Mooring Hitch

Page: 159

58. Marlinespike Hitch

Also known as: Marlingspike Hitch

This is a Slipped Overhand Knot (p.49) with a shaft passed through the drawloop to provide a temporary handle with which to pull the line. It can be used with heavy rope, but its main use is to apply tension on thin stuff that would otherwise cut into your hands. It's especially useful for pulling thread tight in whippings and seizings (see Part Nine). A screwdriver or any other smooth rod can be used in place of a proper marlinespike.

Uses: adding a temporary "handle" for pulling thin cordage

Pros: quick and easy, unties instantly; adds power and comfort when pulling

Cons: strictly temporary; can slip in use

Instructions

1. Make an underhand crossing turn

2. Position the standing part beneath the crossing turn to make a "pretzel" shape.

Untying: Remove the marlinespike. The knot becomes a Slipped Overhand Knot that can be easily pulled straight.

Marline, Marling, Marlin
Marline (also marling and marlin) is thin, strong cord, usually tarred, used for seizings and servings on sailing ships. The word has a confused etymology but it clearly has nothing to do with the marlin fish. A marlinespike is a tool to pull marline tight, and marlinespike seamanship refers to this kind of work, in addition to splicing.

3. Pass the marlinespike over-under-over through the crossing turn: over the top of the crossing turn, under the standing part, and over the bottom of the crossing turn.

4. Pull the marlinespike so that it draws a bight into the standing part that comes through the crossing turn from back to front. Continue pulling until the crossing turn tightens against the marlinespike.

59. **Round Turn and Two Half Hitches**

One of the best hitches for loads that are roughly perpendicular to a fixed object, Two Half Hitches are easy to tie and untie, fairly secure, adjustable for tightness or length, and stronger than most hitches, because the load is born by the turns around the object, not by the knot itself. The preferred method begins with a round turn around the object.

Uses: hitch for any load perpendicular to object; boats, clotheslines, ridge lines, towing, tent guys

Pros: strong, secure, easy to tie and untie, adjustable

Cons: not as secure as a Taut Line Hitch

Instructions

1. Make a round turn around the object. If the object is vertical, it is often more convenient, but not essential, to wind the round turn downward, so that the working end finishes below the standing part.

2. Make an overhand crossing turn around the standing part to form the first Half Hitch (p.156).

Untying: If the line is loaded, slide the hitches toward the fixed object to release tension. Then undo the Half Hitches.

3. Begin the second Half Hitch by taking the working end in front of the standing part again.

4. Complete the second Half Hitch by making another overhand crossing turn around the standing part.

5. Note how the working end is captured between the two crossing turns.

6. To tighten the standing part, slide the Half Hitches away from the anchoring object, feeding slack through the round turn as needed.

60. Turn and Two Half Hitches

Also known as: Half Turn and Two Half Hitches

Uses: hitch for any load perpendicular to object

Pros: strong, fairly secure, easy to tie and untie

Cons: less secure than a Round Turn with Two Half Hitches

This slightly simpler way to tie Two Half Hitches places a single turn—not a round turn—around the fixed object. It's marginally quicker to tie, requires less rope if it is to be tied around a large object like a tree trunk, and generates less friction against the object, making it less secure but easier to adjust for tension.

Untying: If the line is loaded, slide the hitches toward the fixed object to release tension. Then undo the Half Hitches.

Instructions

1. Take a turn around the fixed object and complete a Half Hitch (p.56).

2. Complete the second Half Hitch.

3. Slide the completed knot toward the working part to take up the slack, feeding line around the fixed object.

4. Or snug the completed knot against the fixed object for slack in the standing part and greater security in the knot itself.

61. Taut Line Hitch

Also known as: Midshipman's Hitch, Blackwall's Hitch

This sliding knot is a little more complicated than Two Half Hitches (p.143), but it holds better. It's a favorite among canoeists and other small boaters to tighten the boat's bow and stern lines to a car's towing hooks when car-topping.

Uses: adjustable hitch; tent and fly guys, roof-rack cargo tie-down, clotheslines, tarp ridgelines

Pros: tightens easily; holds better than Two Half Hitches

Cons: can slip

Instructions

1. Tie a Half Hitch (p.56) around or through the fixed object.

Untying: Slide the knot along the standing part to create some slack, then undo the final Half Hitch to free the working end.

2. Lift the working end to make an overhand crossing turn around the standing part, then pass the working end behind the standing part.

3. Bring the working end through the half hitch from back to front without overlapping the crossing turn (i.e., keep the working end farther from the fixed object than the crossing turn).

4. The working end pulled tight at this stage.

5. Pass the working end behind the standing part and bring it forward again.

6. Pass the working end under itself to complete a Half Hitch around the standing part.

7. The knot resists slipping when load is applied to the standing part. It can be slid toward the standing part to tighten the line, or slid the other way to snug up against the fixed object and put slack in the standing part.

62. **Buntline Hitch**

The Buntline Hitch holds exceptionally well when snugged up against the object to which it's tied, which makes it a favorite in jobs where the knot will be subjected to a lot of shaking about, like flag halyards and dining flies. It can also be used as a friction noose, like Two Half Hitches (p.143), to tighten the stake end of guylines on tents and flies.

Uses: sail and flag halyards, sail sheets, tarps set flying, friction noose for guylines

Pros: very secure

Cons: difficult to untie

Instructions

1. Make a turn with the working end around the fixed object or through the ring from back to front. Make an overhand crossing turn in the working end around the standing part. Cross the working end over the standing-part leg of the turn.

2. Pass the working end under the standing-part leg of the turn and pull it through to tie a Half Knot (p.55).

3. Push the Half Knot and the crossing turn together, capturing the working end between them, then pull the working end tight. As shown, the knot functions as a friction noose.

Untying: It may be necessary to create slack in the standing part first. Then slide the knot toward the standing part to create slack around the object. At that point, the working end can be pulled free.

4. If the knot is snugged up tight against the ring, it will hold tenaciously and become very difficult to untie.

63. Anchor Bend—Version 1

Also known as: Fisherman's Bend

In spite of its name, the Anchor Bend is a hitch, and it is usually tied to a ring. It is ideal for tying an anchor, because the initial round turn is not tightened around the anchor's ring. This loose connection allows the knot to shift in compensation to a boat's continual movements when at anchor, reducing strain on the rope.

Uses: anchors, grapnels, hitching to any ring
Pros: very secure; does not tighten against the hitched object; holds well in slippery line
Cons: none known

Instructions

Untying: Undo the Half Hitch, then pull the working end through the round turn. If you can't pull the working end through, loosen the round turn by pulling slack from the standing part.

1. Pass the working end through the ring from back to front, then through again to make a round turn. Pass the working end behind the standing part.

2. Pass the working end through the round turn.

3. The working end may be pulled tight at this point, as shown, if you want the knot to be solid against the ring. If you want the knot to "float" around the ring, leave it loose for now.

4. Pass the working end behind the standing part, bring it forward, and pass it through to make a single Half Hitch (p.56) around the standing part.

5. Pull the Half Hitch tight against the round turn.

64. **Anchor Bend—Version 2**

Unlike the standard Anchor Bend (p.147), this version does not "float." It needs to be tightened against the ring. What it gives up in strain reduction it gains in lower abrasion.

Uses: anchors, grapnels, hitching to any ring

Pros: strong, secure, compact; lower abrasion than standard Anchor Bend

Cons: applies more strain to rope than a standard Anchor Bend

Instructions

Untying: Pull the working end through the round turn. If necessary, first loosen the round turn by pulling slack from the standing part through the doubled Half Hitch.

1. Pass the working end through the ring from front to back, then through again to make a round turn. Pass the working end in front of the standing part then through the round turn to make a kind of doubled Half Hitch (p.56). Don't pull it tight yet.

2. Take the working end across and in front of the round turn.

3. Pass the working end through the round turn a second time. The knot must be worked gradually into shape, pulling slack through the round turn and hitches and into the working end and standing parts a bit at a time until the round turn is tight around the ring.

65. Clove Hitch

Also known as: Builder's Knot, Dry Weather Hitch

This is a useful light-duty hitch for situations where the load will be fairly constant and at right angles to a stationary object, but it can be insecure—or it may jam—in other situations. It's easy to tie in the end of a rope, as described here, or on a bight, as shown on the following page. It forms the basis for several other hitches and can also serve as a light-duty binding knot.

Uses: light-duty hitch, tying up boats, hanging gear from horizontal poles, binding knot

Pros: easy and quick to tie

Cons: insecure; can jam

Instructions

2. Pass the working end underneath itself, beside the standing part. To make the knot easier to untie, the working end may be formed into a bight before passing it through, to make a drawloop.

1. Form a Single Hitch (p.54) with the working end over the standing part. Bring the working end around the object again but do not pull it tight.

Untying: Pull the working end through the first Single Hitch that secures it, then through the second one.

3. Pull both ends to tighten.

66. **Clove Hitch on a Bight**

Also known as: Builder's Knot, Dry Weather Hitch

It is sometimes convenient to tie a Clove Hitch (p.149) on a bight—for example, if the working end is especially long. This method places the rope in its final arrangement before it is slipped over one end of the object, but it results in a knot that's a proper Clove Hitch.

Uses: light-duty hitch, tying up boats, perimeter lines on stakes, binding knot

Pros: easy and quick to tie

Cons: insecure; can jam

Instructions

Untying: Loosen both Single Hitches by pulling some slack from both ends, then slip the knot off the end of the object.

1. In a bight of the rope, make an underhand and an overhand crossing turn next to each other.

2. Place the underhand crossing turn over the overhand crossing turn.

3. Slide both crossing turns over an end of the object

4. Pull both ends to tighten.

67. **Constrictor Knot**

Also known as: Gunner's Knot

The Constrictor Knot is far more secure as a hitch than the closely related Clove Hitch (p.149) and is one of the best binding knots around. It excels in thin line and makes a very effective seizing in the end of a heavier rope to prevent unraveling. If pulled tight, it can be nearly impossible to untie.

Uses: heavy-duty hitch in thin line, binding, seizing

Pros: very secure; easy to tie; ends can be cut short

Cons: very difficult to untie

Instructions

1. Tie a loose Clove Hitch around the object.

2. Lift the standing part where it begins to make a turn around the object and tuck the working end through.

Untying: If the knot has been pulled tight, it may be impossible to untie. To cut safely, apply your knife to the top diagonal part.

3. Pull both ends tight.

68. Rolling Hitch

Also known as: Magnus Hitch, Magner's Hitch

Where the Clove Hitch (p.149) only works well when the load is at nearly a right angle to the object, this cousin knot holds securely when the load and the object are in or near alignment with each other. It therefore works well to hoist spars, pilings, and other poles in a vertical orientation.

Uses: lifting or securing a load in the same direction as a shaft or line, taking strain off another rope, pulling or securing another rope

Pros: secure and easy

Cons: only secure with load in line with object

Instructions

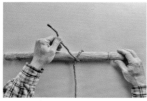

1. Make a Single Hitch (p.54) around the object or other rope with the working end over the standing part. Ultimately, load will be applied by the standing part from the direction in which the working end overlaps the standing part at this stage (i.e., from the right in the photo).

2. Make a turn around the object, bringing the working end between the standing part and the crossing turn.

3. Make another turn around the object, this time over the standing part to capture it a second time.

4. Bring the working end under the previous turn, forming a Half Knot (p.55). The working end may be formed into a bight to create a drawloop if desired.

5. Pull both ends to tighten. When load is applied in the proper direction, the standing part will overlap the two turns to the right, not the working end.

69. **Timber Hitch**

The timber and construction industries use the Timber Hitch regularly for hauling and lifting logs, poles, pilings, and culvert tubes. It cannot be tied tightly around the object, but when load is applied, the pressure of the rope against the object secures it well, and when the load is released, the knot becomes loose again and is easy to undo.

Uses: hauling, lifting or towing logs, pipes, heavy objects, or bundles of poles

Pros: simple to tie and untie

Cons: insecure if load is perpendicular to object; may require turning the object

Instructions

1. Make an underhand crossing turn around the object a little way back from the end from which the object will be pulled.

2. Bring the working end forward to form an overhand crossing turn around the standing part.

3. Tuck the working end underneath the crossing turn that surrounds the object.

Untying: Simply unwrap the working end through the tucks.

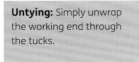

4. Make at least two more tucks around the first crossing turn. More tucks will be more secure.

5. Pull the standing part tight and haul the load from the standing part.

70. Cow Hitch

Also known as: Lark's Head, Lanyard Hitch, Ring Hitch, Tag Hitch, Bale Sling Hitch

The panoply of alternate names for the Cow Hitch hints at its popularity in different trades. It's a quick, easy way to add a loop or a pair of tie-off points to a fixed object, and it can be tied by several methods, at the end of a rope or on a bight. As long as both working ends are secure, it can't come undone.

Uses: hitching animals, hanging gear, adding loops or tie-offs to posts, rails, rings, or other ropes

Pros: simple and quick to tie by many methods; easy to untie; does not jam

Cons: insecure; slips under unequal loads

Method 1: On a Bight

Use this method when both working ends are free and will be tied to the object being secured after the hitch is in place.

1. Double the rope, making a bight at the halfway point. Pass the bight through or around the fixed object.

2. Pass both working ends through the bight.

3. Pull both working ends tight to finish the hitch.

71. Method 2: In a Sling

This is a convenient method to add a loop to a fixed object for hanging gear. It's quite similar to the previous method.

1. Form a bight in the sling and pass it through or around the object.

2. Pass the rest of the sling through the bight and pull it tight.

Untying: If both working ends are free, simply grab the crossing part and pull. If only one working end is free, pull on the turn in the standing part to draw the free working end through the crossing part. If both ends are to remain tied, pull some slack into the standing parts, then pull the slack into the crossing part: the knot can then be slid over the end of the fixed object.

72. Method 3: Over the End

This is a convenient method for hitching to an open-ended object. It works with two free ends or with a closed loop. It's an effective way to tie a horse's closed reins to a stake or post.

1. Make a bight in the rope, then fold the bight over the two standing parts to form two overhand crossing turns, one clockwise and the other counterclockwise.

2. Fold the two crossing turns back around the standing parts.

3. Slide the crossing turns over the end of the fixed object and pull the standing parts tight.

73. Method 4: With One Working End

This method is used when one of the rope's ends is already attached to the object being secured, but the other end is free.

1. Make an overhand crossing turn around the fixed object. Pass the working end behind the object. (The working end is short in the photo for clarity. It would normally be as long as the standing part.)

2. Bring the working end forward and down, adjacent and parallel to the standing part. This creates an underhand crossing turn next to the overhand one.

3. Pull both ends tight, then attach the free working end to the object to be restrained.

74. Pedigree Cow Hitch

All other Cow Hitches have two standing parts, both of which must be loaded fairly equally. In contrast, the Pedigree Cow Hitch is designed to be tied with a short working end, and to bear load on a single standing part. It's often recommended for hanging garden tools from a horizontal pole (with the standing part of the rope permanently attached to the tool handle), but it's fairly secure no matter what direction the pull is from.

Uses: hitching to rails, posts and rings, hanging gear

Pros: the only cow hitch for load on one standing part; secure in any direction; easy to tie

Cons: not among the most secure hitches; can be difficult to untie

Instructions

Untying: If the hitch is too tight to pull the working end free, pull slack from the standing part through the bight, then loosen the bight and the crossing turn that secures the working end.

1. Make a bight near the working end of the rope and pass it through the ring from back to front or behind the object to which it will be tied.

2. Pass both ends of the rope through the bight, forming two crossing turns around the object. (If either end is not available, follow the first two steps of Cow Hitch, Method 4, p.155.)

3. Pass the working end through both crossing turns.

4. Pull the working end tight, then pull the standing part to tighten the knot.

75. **Cow Hitch with a Toggle**

Sometimes a Cow Hitch is desired and none of the previous methods apply, because the fixed object is closed (like a ring), neither end of the rope is free, and the object being restrained is too large or unwieldy to pass through a bight. This hitch relies on a toggle —a short stick or shaft of some sort—to hold. It's an excellent method by which gear with a hanging loop already attached can be hung from a horizontal line.

Uses: hanging gear from rings and horizontal ropes or rails

Pros: quick and easy to tie and untie; works when only a bight is available

Cons: insecure if subject to motion; will slip if loaded unevenly; requires a toggle

Instructions

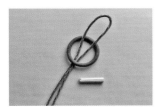

Untying: Pull out the toggle and the bight can be withdrawn from the fixed object.

1. Pass the bight through the ring or around the fixed object.

2. Bend the bight down over the two standing parts to make two opposed crossing turns.

3. Slip the toggle through both crossing turns, going over, under, under, and over the legs in order.

4. Pull the standing parts to secure the toggle.

76. Mooring Hitch

Also known as: High Post Hitch

This hitch is used to tie a boat to a bollard, tree, or post on a shoreline high above the water, especially useful in locks and areas of wide tidal change. If the working end is left long, the knot can be instantly released from the deck. When released, the rope remains around the bollard, until you release the working end and pull it all the way off.

Uses: quick-release adjustable hitch for constant light loads

Pros: releases instantly and adjustable far from the fixed object

Cons: rather insecure

Instructions

1. Take a turn around the fixed object. Make an underhand crossing turn in the working end and position it over the standing part. Make a bight in the remaining working end just below the crossing turn. (The loop around the object has been made short in the photograph for clarity; in practice, make it long enough so that the knot is close to the boat.)

2. Place the bight over-under-over through the crossing turn. The first two parts of that maneuver are shown here: over the standing-part leg of the crossing turn and under the main standing part of the rope.

3. As the final part of the over-under-over maneuver, the bight is pulled over the opposite leg of the crossing turn. You have just tied a Marlinespike Hitch (p.141), using the bight in place of the spike.

4. In one hand hold the working end against the other leg of the bight where it crosses the turn around the object, and pull the standing part of the rope to tighten the knot. Slide the knot along the standing part to take up or let out slack. Pulling on the working end will instantly release the knot.

Untying: Simply pull the working end and the knot comes apart.

77. Highwayman's Hitch

The Highwayman's Hitch can be instantly released from a point far from the object to which it is tied. But unlike the Mooring Hitch (opposite), which shares this feature, the Highwayman's Hitch is snugged against the object, and when released the rope is completely free of the object and does not have to be pulled from around it, allowing a quicker getaway, be it in a canoe or on a horse.

Uses: quick-release hitch for boats or horses

Pros: releases instantly far from the fixed object

Cons: rather insecure; not adjustable like the Mooring Hitch

Instructions

1. Make a bight in the working end and pass it around the fixed object, leaving the working end of the bight behind the object. Make another bight in the standing part. (The working end has been left short in the photograph for clarity, but leave it long enough to reach the boat, horse, or whatever at the far end.)

2. Pass the second bight through the first one from back to front.

3. Make a third bight in the working end.

Untying: Pull the working end and the knot is immediately free of the fixed object.

4. Pass it through the second bight from back to front.

5. Holding the third bight, pull the standing part to tighten the knot.

Part Eight
Lashings and Special-purpose Knots

Camp structures and emergency shelters rely on lashings to tie poles together in various configurations. Such structures are often lashed with relatively light cord, and a lot of cordage is needed to make a lashing that will bear much weight and retain rigidity. The other knots in this section are specific to climbers, boaters, and anyone carrying cargo on top of a vehicle or on a trailer.

78. Square Lashing

Uses: binding poles at right angles

Pros: very secure

Cons: time-consuming to tie and untie; uses a lot of cordage

Page: 162

79. Diagonal Lashing

Uses: binding diagonal braces

Pros: very secure

Cons: time-consuming to tie and untie; uses a lot of cordage

Page: 164

80. Sheer Lashing

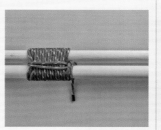

Uses: lashing poles lengthwise; extending pole length

Pros: very strong and secure

Cons: time-consuming to tie and untie; uses a lot of cordage

Page: 166

81. Pole Lashing

Uses: lashing poles for carrying

Pros: quick and secure

Cons: may require cutting short lengths of rope

Page: 168

82. Slip Knot Trucker's Hitch

Uses: tying cargo on vehicles, securing tarps over stacked material

Pros: tight, secure, adjustable

Cons: uses a lot of rope; may be difficult to untie

Page: 170

83. Sheepshank

Uses: shortening a line; bypassing a worn section, slinging a ladder

Pros: strong, secure under constant load

Cons: insecure if subjected to movement

Page: 172

84. Cleat Hitch

Uses: tying boats; securing halyards, sail sheets, and boat fenders

Pros: easy to tie and untie; secure

Cons: none known

Page: 174

85. Prusik Knot

Uses: moveable handholds, tie-offs, or clip-on points on climbing rope

Pros: quick, easy, fairly secure

Cons: only secure under load; can slip if wet or icy

Page: 176

86. Klemheist Knot

Uses: moveable handholds, tie-offs, or clip-on points on climbing rope

Pros: more secure than Prusik Knot

Cons: only secure under load

Page: 177

87. Italian Hitch

Uses: climbing: belaying, braking, rappelling

Pros: flexible, multi-purpose slide-and-lock hitch

Cons: kinks; can ruin rope when rappelling

Page: 178

78. **Square Lashing**

Use this lashing to connect a vertical and horizontal pole at right angles to each other for shelters, platforms, scaffolds, and ladders. The connection will be solid and the horizontal pole will bear a great deal of weight.

Uses: binding poles at right angles

Pros: very secure

Cons: time-consuming to tie and untie; uses a lot of cordage

Instructions

1. Position yourself on the side of the structure so that the vertical pole is in front of the horizontal one. Tie a Clove Hitch (p.149) around the vertical pole, just beneath the horizontal one.

2. Pass the working end behind the horizontal pole at the 3:00 position, in front of the vertical pole at 12:00, then back behind the horizontal one at 9:00. When you pull the rope tight after passing it behind the horizontal pole the first time, the clove hitch may slip around the pole as shown: this is OK.

3. Continue wrapping the rope in the same counterclockwise direction around the crossing, going behind the horizontals and in front of the verticals. Wrap the rope next to, not over, the previous wrap, and pull it as tight as possible with each turn. Make three full wraps all the way around. (The starting Clove Hitch makes it appear that there are more than three wraps at the 6:00 position.)

4. Make a round turn behind the horizontal pole at the 3:00 position.

5. Working now in a clockwise direction, pass the rope behind the verticals and in front of the horizontals. Pulling the rope very tight with each of these frapping turns will further tighten the first set of wraps.

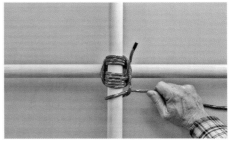

6. Make three full frapping turns.

7. After the last frapping turn, make a Half Hitch (p.56) below the wraps on the vertical pole at 6:00.

Untying: Undo the final Clove Hitch, then unwrap all the frapping turns and round turns around the poles, ending by untying the first Clove Hitch.

8. Pass the rope around the vertical pole one more time and complete a final Clove Hitch.

79. **Diagonal Lashing**

Most perpendicular structures require diagonal bracing to remain square: without it, they're likely to collapse parallelogram-wise. After lashing a structure's main horizontal and vertical members with Square Lashings (p.162), add diagonal braces from corner to corner. Use Diagonal Lashings where the diagonals cross verticals and horizontals, and where the diagonals cross each other.

Uses: binding diagonal braces to each other and to horizontal and vertical members

Pros: very secure

Cons: time-consuming to tie and untie; uses a lot of cordage

Instructions

1. Tie a Timber Hitch (p.153) vertically around both poles, with both ends finishing up on top of the pole closer to you and the long working end facing downward.

2. Make three round turns around both poles in the same direction, pulling each turn very tight. The round turns will go right over the Timber Hitch, but should not overlap each other.

Untying: Undo the final Clove Hitch, then unwrap all the frapping turns and round turns around the poles, ending by untying the Timber Hitch.

3. Take the working end behind the pole that's closer to you, working counterclockwise.

79. **Diagonal Lashing**

4. Pass the working end over the first set of round turns and horizontally across the crossing of the poles.

5. Make three full adjacent round turns around both poles in the same direction, pulling each turn very tight.

6. After the third horizontal round turn, shift the working end downward and begin making frapping turns counterclockwise between the two poles and over the two sets of round turns. Make three full frapping turns, pulling each one very tight.

7. Finish the lashing with a clove hitch around the back pole.

80. Sheer Lashing

This lashing is used when you need a shaft longer than your longest pole. For light-duty use, such as an improvised fishing rod, a single Sheer Lashing may suffice to splice the overlapped ends of two thin sapling poles together. But for structural members like vertical supports on signal towers, flag staffs, or ridge beams, the poles should have considerable overlap and lashings at both ends.

Uses: lashing poles lengthwise; extending pole length

Pros: very strong and secure

Cons: time-consuming to tie and untie; uses a lot of cordage

Instructions

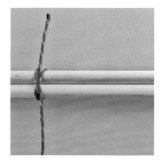

1. Tie a Clove Hitch (p.149) around both poles, leaving a very long working end.

2. Fold the short standing part between the two poles. Take the working end around both poles to hold the standing part in place.

3. Make a series of round turns around both poles, until the wrapping is twice as long as the combined diameters of the poles. Make the wraps snug but not so tight that you can't sneak the rope between the poles for the next step.

A-frame Lashing

The Sheer Lashing is also the basis for building a sturdy fork or A-frame for a shelter gable, a bucking horse, a teepee frame, or similar structure. Place two equal-length poles side by side and tie a Sheer Lashing, but leave the frapping turns and wrappings relatively loose. The bottoms of the poles can then be spread out so that the poles form an X, the top angle of which can support a horizontal pole. It can also be used as a two-man lifting device to raise a mast or a beam.

Untying: Undo the final Clove Hitch, then unwrap the frapping turns and round turns around the poles, ending by untying the first Clove Hitch.

4. Make a turn (not a round turn) around one of the poles and pass the working end between them.

5. Bring the working end down to the opposite end of the wraps and pull it back between the two poles. Pull this frapping turn tight.

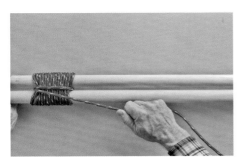

6. Make a second frapping turn and pull it tight.

7. Tie a Half Hitch (p.56) around the pole opposite the one that took a turn before the frapping turns began.

8. Bring the working end around the same pole and complete a Clove Hitch.

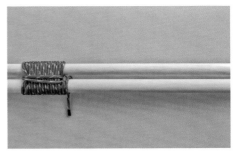

9. Complete the lashing by tucking the working end between the poles one more time.

81. Pole Lashing

This is an excellent knot for tying together bundles of poles or other long, narrow objects for carrying, because the initial bights snug the poles together tightly before they're secured with a Square Knot (p.76). Tie a lashing at each end of a bundle of canoe or kayak paddles, tent poles, skis and ski poles, long sticks of firewood, or poles for shelters.

Uses: lashing poles for carrying

Pros: secure

Cons: may require cutting short lengths of rope

Instructions

1. Working on the ground next to the poles that will be lashed, arrange short lengths of rope into two bights facing opposite directions. It doesn't matter if the ropes form S or Z shapes, as shown at the right and left.

2. Lay the poles over the ropes so that an end and a bight are accessible on each side. Take one rope end and pass it through the bight on the opposite side of the poles.

Untying: Untie the Square Knot by pulling the working ends through the top Half Knot.

3. Take the other rope end and pass it through the other bight.

4. Pull the ends firmly down and away from each other. This will shift the bights toward the bottom of the bundle.

5. Tie a Half Knot (p.55) with the two ends.

6. Tie another Half Knot in the opposite direction to complete a Square Knot.

7. The completed lashing.

8. Completed Pole Lashings at both ends of the bundle.

82. **Slip Knot Trucker's Hitch**

An effective lashing is essential when tying boats or gear to a car's roof rack. Various knots go by the name "Trucker's Hitch," but they all follow the principle of this version: after tying off the standing end, the working end goes over the load then down and around the second tie-off point, then up through a loop knot in the standing part and back down, where it is tied off to itself with a sliding hitch.

Uses: tying gear to roof racks or trailers; securing tarps over stacked material

Pros: tight, secure, adjustable

Cons: uses a lot of rope; slip knot may be difficult to untie

Instructions

1. Imagine that the standing part of the rope (out of the photograph to the top) has already been tied to a fixed point on the opposite side of the vehicle with a Bowline (p.100). The rope has then been thrown over the load and we're about to tie down on this side. Begin with an overhand crossing turn.

2. Make a bight just below the crossing turn and pass it through from back to front.

Untying: Slide the Taut Line Hitch up to create slack, then undo the final Half Hitch (p.56) to free the working end and unravel the rest of it. Pull the working end through the loop knot, remove it from the second tie-off point, then pull it sharply to remove the loop from the Slipped Overhand Knot.

3. Pull down on the bight to complete a Slipped Overhand Knot (p.49). This provides purchase—a point where mechanical advantage can be exerted, much like on a pulley.

4. Bring the working end around the attachment point on the near side of the vehicle, then thread it through the drawloop of the Slipped Overhand Knot.

5. Haul down hard on the working end, then tie it to itself between the Slipped Overhand Knot and the attachment point using a Taut Line Hitch (p.144).

Right: A Bowline (shown) is a good knot to begin the tie-down process. A Slip Knot Trucker's Hitch secures the canoe to the roof rack crossbar on the other side of the car. Similar knot combinations should be used on both crossbars, and from the bow and stern of the canoe to the front and rear bumpers or tow hooks on the vehicle.

Boats and Roof Racks

At highway speeds, the wind can exert hundreds of pounds of force against a boat on a vehicle's roof rack. Add in the jolting that is likely to occur along the typical access road to the put-in, and the need for a really secure tie-down system becomes clear. Canoes, sea kayaks, and rowboats should have a minimum of three tie-downs: one across the boat at each end of the roof rack, and a third from the bow of the boat to the front bumper, a tie-off point under the hood, or a towing loop beneath the front of the vehicle. A fourth line, from the boat's stern to a suitable point on the back of the vehicle, is also advisable. All should be high-quality rope that holds knots securely (not cheap clothesline or hollow-braid polypropylene). Shoving against a properly secured boat should rock the vehicle on its suspension without shifting the boat on the rack. Beware, however, of pulling the lines so tight as to damage the boat or the vehicle. Protect the car's finish by padding bow and stern lines with a rag or a piece of foam pipe insulation where they press against the bodywork.

83. **Sheepshank**

Also known as: Dog Shank

The Sheepshank is useful to shorten a line. For example, when lashing a tarp over a load on a trailer, a Sheepshank can be used to take up any excess length of rope, so that only a sufficient length of working end has to be pulled through the purchase of a Trucker's Hitch (p.170). It's also a good way to bypass a weak or worn section of rope if you don't want to cut it out.

Uses: shortening a line; bypassing a worn section; loop knot with two fixed loops

Pros: very strong; secure under constant load

Cons: insecure if subjected to movement or irregular loading

Instructions

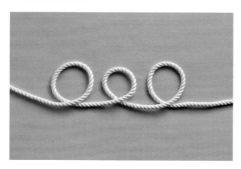

1. Make three underhand counterclockwise crossing turns.

2. Reach through the back of the left crossing turn and grab the left leg of the middle crossing turn.

Untying: With load off the rope, pull the part of the original middle crossing turn that runs directly between the left and right crossing turns, so that the loops are drawn through the crossing turns.

3. Reach through the front of the right crossing turn and grab the right leg of the middle crossing turn.

Sheepshank refinements: If the Sheepshank is being used to bypass a weak section of rope, the weak section should be at the top of the middle crossing turn in Step 1. When the knot is tightened, the weak section will run directly between the tightened crossing turns to the right and left and will not be a part of either of them. The size of the crossing turns can be varied to take up more length of rope (make the middle crossing turn larger) or to make a pair of larger loops (make the right and left crossing turns larger).

4. Pulling outward with both hands, pull both legs of the middle crossing turn through the left and right crossing turns.

5. Continue pulling on the expanded middle crossing turn until the outer crossing turns tighten down around it.

6. Pull both ends of the rope to finish tightening the knot.

7. The finished Sheepshank.

84. **Cleat Hitch**

Cleats provide convenient tie-off points on boats, docks, flagpoles, truck racks, boat hoists, and elsewhere. Tying the knot should be equally convenient: quick, secure, and easy to untie no matter how much load is on the line. This common method, which has no recognized name, fills the bill with none of the superfluous wraps one so often sees.

Uses: tying boats in slips and at docks; securing halyards, sheets and fenders; flag halyards

Pros: easy to tie and untie; secure

Cons: none known

Instructions

1. Most cleats are mounted at an oblique angle to the direction of the line. Run the line under the far horn of the cleat so that it does not pass beneath the near horn. Do not run the line all the way around the base of the cleat.

2. Take the line over the top of the cleat, then underneath the near horn in the same direction that it passed under the far one. (In other words: if the line passes under the far horn from right to left, as shown, it should also pass under the near horn from right to left.)

Untying: Pull the working end through the Single Hitch, then unwrap it from the horns of the cleat.

3. Make an overhand crossing turn in the working end.

4. Turn the crossing turn over so that it becomes an underhand crossing turn. Place it over the far horn of the cleat.

5. Pull the working end tight, completing a Single Hitch (p.54).

6. The finished knot consists of two underhand crossing turns. The working end is parallel and adjacent to the underhand leg of the crossing turn on the near horn. The overhand leg of the near crossing turn holds down the working end. For additional security, another underhand crossing turn may be added to the near horn. This is especially important if the cleat is mounted vertically and the second overhand crossing turn is around the bottom horn of the cleat.

85. **Prusik Knot**

Climbers use the Prusik Knot to create moveable tie-off points on a vertical climbing rope. Tied with a sling around the main climbing rope, it can be easily slid up or down to reposition a carabiner or serve as a hand- or foot-hold. The sling grasps the climbing rope only when load is applied up or down. The rope of the sling should be no more than half the diameter of the main rope.

Uses: climbing; handholds, tie-offs or clip-on points; whitewater rescue; purchase on an anchor rope

Pros: quick, easy; secure in most situations

Cons: only secure under load; can slip if wet or icy

Instructions

1. Make a bight in the sling, pass it behind the main rope, and pass the rest of the sling through the bight, forming a loose Cow Hitch (p.154).

2. Grab the sling at the opposite end from the bight and form it into a second bight.

3. Pass the new bight between the main rope and the crossing part of the Cow Hitch.

Untying: With load off, pull the bight through the crossing part, pull it around the anchoring rope or pole, then pull it through a second time.

4. Pull the new bight through so that the sling makes two round turns around the main rope both above and below the bight.

5. Pull the bight tight to close up the round turns around the main rope. Pulling down on the free part of the sling will cause it to grip the main rope. With load off the sling, the round turns can be slid up or down the main rope.

86. Klemheist Knot

The Klemheist Knot is known as a "Prusiking knot," because it slides and grips like a Prusik (opposite). It works well with a sling that is made of rope at least half the diameter of the main rope, or with tubular tape, and is said to be more secure than a Prusik Knot.

Uses: climbing; moveable handholds or clip-on points on climbing rope

Pros: more secure than Prusik Knot

Cons: none known

Instructions

Untying: Pull the second bight out of the first bight, then pull to unwind the sling from the main rope.

1. Make a bight in the sling and pass it behind the main rope.

2. Wrap the bight up the main rope, making four or five round turns and leaving a short loop.

3. Make a bight in the other end of the sling and pass it through the bottom of the loop.

4. Pull down on the second bight to lock the sling onto the main rope. The knot can be easily slid up or down the main rope when it is unloaded.

87. Italian Hitch

Also known as: Sliding Ring Hitch, Munter Friction Hitch

This knot pays out slack in a controlled manner through a carabiner to the loaded leg, and readily locks up when tension is applied to the other end. It's useful as a safety rope for descending, where the climber himself or an assistant can control the braking end of the line. It can be used for rappelling, but it's very hard on rope and should only be used in a pinch. It can also be used to lower heavy loads where a pulley is not available.

Uses: climbing: belaying, braking, rappelling

Pros: flexible, multi-purpose slide-and-lock hitch

Cons: kinks; can ruin rope if it runs too fast

Instructions

1. Make two crossing turns in the bight of the rope, with an underhand cross on the left and an overhand cross on the right.

2. Fold the crossing turns back to back.

3. Once they are folded together, the left crossing turn becomes a bight.

4. Keeping them side by side, place the bight, then the remaining crossing turn, on the carabiner.

5. Both ends pulled tight. The leg of the crossing turn bears the load; the leg of the bight is the braking or control leg. Pulling the braking leg tightens the crossing turn around the loaded leg and prevents it from feeding out slack.

Part Nine
Whipping and Seizing

There are many ways to prevent the end of a rope from unraveling (see p.34), but whipping is by far the most effective. Whipping involves binding the rope's strands or yarns with a tight wrapping of heavy thread or light twine. This seemingly imposing task is actually quite easy, and after doing it once or twice, you'll find it second nature. Seizing is a similar procedure to permanently join two lengths of rope or sections of the same rope. A seized eye in the end of a rope is stronger, more secure, and more compact than any loop knot.

Common Whipping

Uses: prevent fraying; mark positions on rope

Pros: easy, quick, and effective

Cons: whipping will unravel if the thread breaks

Page: 181

French Whipping

Uses: prevent fraying; mark positions on rope; as service to prevent abrasion

Pros: resists unraveling if cut

Cons: more time-consuming than Common Whipping

Page: 183

Flat Seizing

Uses: eyes; joining ropes for length or doubling; fastening rope to a shaft

Pros: stronger, more secure, uses less rope, and less bulky than knots

Cons: more difficult and time-consuming than knots; cannot be untied

Page: 185

Materials and General Methods

Few tools and materials are required for the whippings and seizing that follow. Here's what you'll need:

Whipping Thread
Also known as whipping twine, this heavy thread is sold by boat chandlers and rigging supply vendors. It is waxed, which helps it stay in position while you're winding it around the rope. For needle-and-thread whipping methods, the wax also helps it pass smoothly through the rope's fibers.

Traditionally (or as far back as synthetic ropes go), one used natural fiber twine for natural fiber rope, and synthetic twine for synthetic rope. Nowadays, most of the thread that is sold for whipping is nylon, and it works well for ropes of either natural or synthetic fiber. It is immensely strong for its diameter so it can be pulled very tight. Nylon also stretches, and if it is pulled tight around the rope while whipping, it will grip tenaciously.

If proper whipping thread is not available, carpet thread or other very heavy synthetic threads will do. These substitutes, however, will not be waxed, and even for the non-needle whipping methods shown here, it is helpful to wax the thread first by drawing it across a block of beeswax or canning wax.

Seizing Twine
Whipping thread is often used for seizing, but tarred marline, which is heavier, is recommended. Seizings are subjected to greater stress than whipping, and when pulled tight enough for a seizing, narrower thread might bite into and cut some of the rope's fibers. Marline is expensive and hard to come by, but braided nylon mason's twine is a good alternative. Available at any builder's supply

store, it is very strong and quite inexpensive. Make sure you get the braided stuff, not twisted.

Knife
Any type will do, as long as it's sharp and straight-bladed, not serrated.

Marlinespike
Whippings and seizings must be pulled so tight that you can't do it bare-handed; the twine will bite you! By tying a Marlinespike Hitch (p.141) around a proper marlinespike, screwdriver, ice pick, or similar object, you can exert all the tension you need.

Electrician's Tape
Tape works better than cordage for temporarily holding the strands together while you whip the end. It's easier to wrap the whipping right up to the edge of the tape. Masking or painter's tape will work in a pinch, but neither can be stretched tight like plastic electrician's tape.

Cutting Board
You'll want something to cut the whipped end against. A scrap of plywood or dimensional lumber will do the job.

Common Whipping

Also known as: Plain Whipping, Ordinary Whipping

This is the easiest whipping to apply, and it is reliable in most applications. Its drawback is that if a single wrap of the thread is worn through or cut, the entire whipping will unravel.

Uses: whipping the end of a rope to prevent fraying; marking positions on a line

Pros: easy, quick, and effective

Cons: if the thread is cut anywhere, the entire whipping will unravel

Instructions

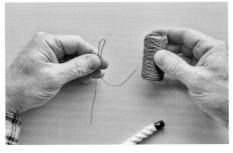

1. Apply electrical tape around the rope just above where you intend to whip it. If the rope is already frayed, apply the tape on a part that is still intact. Cut through the tape to remove the frayed end or excess length of rope.

2. Make a bight near the working end of the whipping thread. This whipping will be easier if you pay the thread directly from the spool, as shown, rather than cutting off the length you will need.

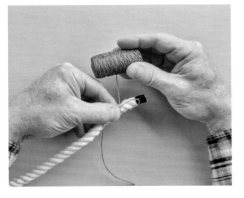

Untying: cannot be untied; must be cut.

3. Lay the bight in the thread against the rope, with the bight overlapping the tape. The bottom of the bight should be one to two times the rope's diameter back from the tape, and you should leave a few inches of working end beyond that—enough to pull on later. (Leave a little more than is shown in the photo.) Wrap the thread directly from the spool around the working end of the bight, making a Single Hitch (p.54) around the rope in the same direction as the lay of the rope.

Common Whipping

4. Take a round turn around the rope and the bight, laying it right against the Single Hitch. Take a second round turn, laying it against the first, working toward the end of the rope. Holding the spool, pull the thread really tight.

5. Continue making round turns, pulling the thread tight and laying each one right against the previous turn. Stop when the wraps cover a length of rope that is between one and two times its diameter. The end of the bight should still be visible, and there should be enough rope exposed between the wraps and the tape to cut through safely.

6. Holding the wraps tight against the rope, cut the thread from the spool, leaving an end longer than the whipping.

7. Pass the newly cut end all the way through the bight.

8. Tie a Marlinespike Hitch (p.141) around a spike in the working end of the bight at the bottom of the whipping. Pull on that end, to bring the eye of the bight under the wraps. It will pull the opposite end of the thread along with it. Stop pulling when the bight is well buried under the wraps. Trim the ends at the top and bottom of the whipping.

9. Cut the rope between the whipping and the tape.

French Whipping

French Whipping is a little more difficult to tie than Common Whipping (p.181), but it is more secure, because each wrap is tied as a Half Hitch (p.56). Should any single wrap be worn through or cut, the rest of the whipping will remain intact. Half Hitches cannot be tied readily from the spool, so the whipping thread must be cut first, allowing a goodly length for pulling and tying the final knots tight.

Uses: whipping the end of a rope to prevent fraying; marking lengths on a line; service

Pros: resists unraveling if cut

Cons: more time-consuming than Common Whipping

Instructions

1. Allowing one to two times the rope's diameter for the whipping, tie a Half Knot (p.55) around the rope with both ends of the whipping thread facing the rope's end. If you are whipping laid rope, the long working end of the thread should face the same direction as the twist toward the end.

2. Align the short standing part of the thread toward the rope's end.

Untying: cannot be untied; must be cut.

3. Tie a Half Hitch in the working end of the thread adjacent to the Half Knot, capturing the short end against the rope.

French Whipping

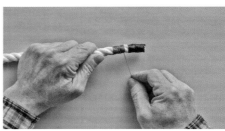

4. Pull the first Half Hitch tight up against the Half Knot. Trim the short end of the thread so that it is a little shorter than the intended length of the whipping.

5. Continue tying Half Hitches, pulling each one very tight right up against the previous one and continuing to bury the thread's short end against the rope.

6. When the wraps cover a length of rope at least equal to its diameter (1.5 times the diameter is better), tie a doubled Half Hitch by making two wraps around the rope before passing the end through both. Pull the knot tight. Make a second doubled Half Hitch and pull it tight.

Serving a Rope

Wrapping twine around a rope to protect it from abrasion is known as serving it, and the resulting ropework is either a serving or service. Service is like whipping, but much longer. Service was used extensively on the standing rigging of sailing ships to prevent abrasion from other pieces of standing or running rigging. A French Whipping several inches in length makes an effective service called a Grapevine Service. In applications where it won't be flexed, it can be painted to enhance its durability.

7. Trim the long end of the thread, trim the short end if any remains exposed, then cut the rope between the whipping and the tape.

8. The stacked Half Hitches confer a spiral pattern to the finished French Whipping.

Flat Seizing

A flat seizing is an extremely effective way to make a loop in the end of a rope, to join two ropes together to extend their length, to double ropes for strength, or to fasten a rope in line with a shaft or pole. The seizing is extremely secure, uses less rope than a knot, and is less bulky and apt to catch on obstructions.

Uses: forming eyes; joining two ropes for length or thickness; fastening rope to a shaft
Pros: compared to knots: stronger, more secure, uses less rope, less bulky
Cons: compared to knots: more difficult, time-consuming, cannot be untied, requires twine

Note
The metal thimble shown in the bight will prevent abrasion if the eye will hold a shackle or bear against a clevis pin, but it is not necessary in many applications.

Untying: cannot be untied; must be cut.

Instructions

1. Leaving the twine on the spool, tie a Constrictor Knot (p.151) around the two pieces of rope to be joined or both legs of a bight (as shown). Position the Constrictor Knot so as to allow the length of the completed seizing to be twice that of the diameter of the rope.

2. Align the short end of the twine between the legs of the bight. Using the spool to pull the twine, begin wrapping round turns around both legs of the rope and the short end of the twine.

3. Place each round turn right up against the previous one, and pull each one as tight as possible.

4. Trim the short end of the twine so that it will be completely covered by the seizing. Keep wrapping until the seizing is twice as long as the rope's diameter.

5. Make a final turn through one leg of the bight, then pull the twine down over the wrappings.

Flat Seizing

6. Bring the end between the legs of the bight and pull it up tight on the other side. Pull the end through the eye, completing the first frapping turn. Then go around again to make another frapping turn.

7. Bring the twine through the eye to complete the second frapping turn. Pass the end under the first frapping turn. A pointed tool can be used to lift this tight frapping turn slightly so that the end can be passed through.

8 Complete a round turn around the first frapping turn, then pass the twine under both frapping turns.

9. Bring the end of the twine through the eye and pull it tight to bring the final knot between the legs of the bight at the base of the eye. Trim the end close.

10. The finished seizing. A second seizing should be added to secure the bitter end to the standing part as shown on p.179.

Glossary

aramid: a synthetic rope fiber often sold under the trade name Kevlar®

bend: a knot which ties the ends of two ropes together

bight: 1. a small-radius curve in a rope in which the working and standing parts are brought near to or in contact with one another; 2. *on the bight:* describing a knot tied in any part of a rope other than the ends

binding knot: a true knot that tightly encloses or binds together another object or objects

bitter end: the last inch or two of a rope's end

bosun's chair: a sling, small suspended platform, or seat used to raise a person up a boat's or ship's mast

breaking strength: the tensile load at which a rope will break under laboratory conditions

bungee, bungee cord: shock cord; cord or rope with a highly elastic core and braided fabric cover, often sold in short, fixed lengths with hooks at both ends

cable: very heavy cordage made up of three twisted *hawsers* (definition 2)

capsize, capsized: a knot that has deformed into a different structure when tightened

chafing gear: any material used to reduce abrasion to a rope

cleat: a piece of hardware with two horn-like extensions to which ropes are hitched

clockwise, counterclockwise: describing the direction of a crossing turn from the standing part to the working end

coil: 1. an arrangement that prevents rope from tangling during storage or transportation; 2. a single loop of rope in a coil

coir: a natural rope fiber from coconut shells

core: the central, strength element of a rope with two-layer construction

crossing turn: a curve in which the rope crosses over itself

drawloop: a bight placed in the working end of a rope just before the final stage of tying a knot, to make it easy to untie. See *slipped*

dynamic use: rope usage in which the load will change

elbow: in a double crossing turn, one of two sections of rope between the crossing turn at the top, and the working end and standing part at the bottom

eye: a small closed loop in a rope's end (or on a bight) formed by seizing or splicing

fair/fairing: to smooth or refine a misshapen knot

fiber: the smallest component, either natural or synthetic, from which cordage is made

fid: a tapered, pointed tool used to loosen knots

foundation knots: an ad-hoc category in this book that introduces basic knots and concepts

frapping turn: in a lashing or seizing, turns of the line over and at a right angle to previous round turns or wrappings, to tighten them

guillotine: a stationary electric hot-knife for cutting rope

halyard: a line used to raise a sail or a flag

hawser: 1. a heavy line, often a cable, for towing, anchoring, or tying up a ship; 2. occasionally: any rope, especially one of three twisted into a cable

heaving line: a rope meant to be thrown

heaving line knot: a stopper knot tied to add weight to the end of a heaving line. Also: the name of a specific heaving line knot.

hemp: a natural rope fiber from the hemp plant (*Cannabis sativa*)

henequen: a natural rope fiber from the henequen agave (*Agave fourcroydes*)

high-modulus polyethylene: a synthetic rope fiber often sold under the trade names Spectra® and Dyneema®

hitch: a knot tied to an object, usually used to connect two objects together with a length of rope between them

jute: a natural rope fiber from plants of the genus *Corchorus*

kernmantle: two-layer rope construction, with a braided cover and a load-bearing core

laid: twisted, describing a method of rope construction

lash, lashing: ropework that ties two or more poles tightly together, usually incorporating numerous round and frapping turns

line: a general term for a rope when it is in use

loop knot: a true knot that forms a closed loop that can be placed around an object

loop: 1. a curve in a rope of a larger radius than a bight that encloses more area than a bight; 2. The part of a loop knot or hitch that goes around an object

manila: a natural rope fiber from the abaca plant (*Musa textillis*); rope of that fiber

mantle: the braided cover of a rope with two-layer construction

middle: to find the mid-point of a rope by folding it in half

monofilament: 1. cordage or a cordage component made from a single, relatively thick fiber of synthetic material; 2. monofilament fishing line

noose: a loop knot in which the size of the loop can be adjusted after the knot is tied

nylon: a synthetic rope fiber, an aliphatic polyamide

overhand: a crossing turn in which the working end is over the standing part

palm, sailmaker's palm: a leather strap with a metal insert, worn on the hand to push needles through rope or canvas

parachute cord (also: *paracord, 550 cord*): small-diameter two-layer synthetic cordage with a braided cover, originally developed for use for parachute suspension, now a common utility cordage

polyester: a synthetic rope fiber often sold under the trade name Dacron®

polyethylene: a synthetic rope fiber

polypropylene: a synthetic rope fiber

purchase: a fixed loop tied on a bight and used like a pulley, to reverse the direction of the working end's pull and increase force when tightening a line

rode: an anchor line

rope: cordage of roughly $\frac{3}{8}$ in. (9 mm) or greater in diameter

round turn: a revolution of rope of 360 to 540 degrees around an object

running end: see *working end*

seize, seizing: a tight wrapping of heavy thread or small cord to join two ropes end-to-end or side-by-side, or to form an eye

service, serving: wrapping of small stuff around a section of rope to prevent abrasion

sheath: see *mantle*

sheet: a line used to control the set of a sail

shock load: a sudden application of force to a rope

shroud: a fixed line that supports a ship's or boat's mast transversely

sisal: a natural rope fiber from the sisal plant (*Agave sisalana*)

S-laid: clockwise twist in the strands of a laid rope, when viewed from an end. See *Z-laid*

sling: a fixed, closed loop of rope, webbing, or tubular tape

slipped: a knot tied with a drawloop to ease untying. See *drawloop*

splice: a structure in which the strands of a rope are separated and then woven together to: terminate a rope; form an eye; or join ropes end-to-end

standing end, standing part: the end of the rope that is not fully subject to manipulation in knot tying

static use: rope usage in which the load force and direction will not change

stay: a line that supports a ship's or boat's mast longitudinally

stop/stopping: small cords tied around a coil of rope to secure it

stopper: a knot used to prevent a line from passing through a small opening

stopper knot: a true knot that prevents a rope end escaping through a small opening, allows it to be thrown, or serves as a hand-hold. Also: the name of a specific stopper knot

strand: 1. a component in cordage made from twisted yarns. Laid ropes consist of strands twisted together; 2. one side of a crossing turn or other knot component; leg

threaded: describing two knots tied in parallel to make a single knot, with the second rope or part following the path of the first rope or part

toggle: a short cylinder of any material used to hold part of a knot in place

top rope: a rope attached to a fixed point to assist climbers below it

true knot: a class of knots in which a rope is tied to itself. True knots include binding, stopper, and loop knots.

turn: a half-revolution of rope around an object

underhand: a crossing turn in which the working end is under the standing part

whip, whipping: 1. a tight wrapping of heavy thread around a rope's end, to prevent it from fraying; 2. any material so applied, such as tape

working end, working part: the free end of a rope that is subject to manipulation in tying a knot

working load: the maximum tensile load considered safe by a rope's manufacturer

wrap: one of several adjacent round turns

yarn: a component in cordage made from twisted fibers; often about the diameter of sewing thread

Z-laid: counterclockwise twist in the strands of a laid rope, when viewed from an end. See *S-laid*

Resources

Books

Ashley, Clifford W., *The Ashley Book of Knots*, Doubleday, 1944

Budworth, Geoffrey, *The Illustrated Encyclopedia of Knots*, Lyons Press, 2000

Budworth, Geoffrey, *The Ultimate Encyclopedia of Knots & Ropework*, Lorenz Books, 1999

Day, Cyrus L., *Knots & Splices*, International Marine, 1953

Owen, Peter, L.L. Bean *Outdoor Knots Handbook*, Lyons Press, 1999

Pawson, Des, *The Handbook of Knots: A Step-By-Step Guide to Tying and Using More Than 100 Knots*, DK Publishing, 1998

Philpott, Lindsey, *Pocket Guide to Knots*, International Marine, 2006

Smith, Hervey Garrett, *The Marlinspike Sailor*, John de Graff, 1971

Spencer, Charles L., and P.W. Blandford (reviser), *Knots, Splices & Fancy Work*, Brown, Son & Ferguson, 1958

Taylor, Roger C., *Knowing the Ropes: Selecting, Rigging, & Handling Lines Aboard*, 2nd edition, International Marine, 1993

Websites

Animated Knots by Grog: www.animatedknots.com

Backcountry.com, page "When to Replace Your Climbing Rope": www.backcountry.com/explore/when-to-replace-your-climbing-rope/

Knots 3D: http://knots3d.com

NetKnots.com: www.netknots.com

Ropers Knots Page: www.realknots.com

Ropework: www.ropebook.com

Scout-Pioneering: Good, Ol'-Fashioned, Outdoor, Scouting Fun for the 21st Century, page "Knot-Tying Terminology": http://scoutpioneering.com/2013/02/11/knot-tying-terminology/

Index

Credits

Bob Holtzman is an outdoorsman, writer, editor, and sporting goods manufacturer. An avid canoeist, he is the author of *The Camping Bible* and *Wilderness Survival Skills: How to Stay Alive in the Wild With Just a Blade & Your Wits*, as well as the *Boats & Ships* series of books for children. He lives in Rockport, Maine, where he runs Mythic Gear (www. MythicDrysuits.com), manufacturing inexpensive drysuits for paddlesports.

Feather Weight is a full service photography studio based in Maine specializing in lifestyle, product, and portrait work. www.feather-weight.com

Other image credits:
p.8 © ueuephoto (Shutterstock); p.9 © Pavelk (Shutterstock); p.10 © aragami12345s (Shutterstock); p.30 © defotoberg (Shutterstock); p.31 © sharky (Shutterstock); p.33 © Csehak Szabolcs (Shutterstock)

Quid Publishing would like to thank Lindsey Philpott at the International Guild of Knot Tyers (www.igk.net) and Glen Nash at the Australian School of Mountaineering (www.climbingadventures.com.au) for their assistance.